Classroom Activities for Correcting Specific Reading Problems

Stephen A. Pavlak, Ph.D.

Professor of Education
California University of Pennsylvania
California, Pennsylvania

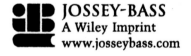
JOSSEY-BASS
A Wiley Imprint
www.josseybass.com

Published by Jossey-Bass
A Wiley Imprint
989 Market Street, San Francisco, CA 94103-1741   www.josseybass.com

Jossey-Bass books and products are available through most bookstores. To contact Jossey-Bass directly
call our Customer Care Department within the U.S. at (800) 956-7739, outside the U.S. at (317) 572-
3986 or fax (317) 572-4002.

Jossey-Bass also publishes its books in a variety of electronic formats. Some content that appears in
print may not be available in electronic books.

Library of Congress Cataloging-in-Publication Data

Pavlak, Stephen A.
      Classroom activities for correcting specific
   reading problems.
      ISBN 0-13-136219-4
      1. Reading—Remedial teaching.   2. Reading games.
   3. Creative activities and seat work.   I. Title.
   LB1050.5.P28   1984   84-19001
   372.4'3

FIRST EDITION
HB Printing 10 9 8 7 6 5 4 3

ABOUT THIS BOOK
OF CORRECTIVE READING ACTIVITIES

The purpose of this book is to give reading specialists and elementary classroom teachers a store of practical, tested activities for correcting specific reading problems and deficiencies. The large number of easy-to-use activities, games, and exercises included provide a diversity of material for meeting students' individual reading needs that have been identified through the use of various standardized and informal diagnostic devices.

The book includes 234 activities in the basic skill areas of phonic analysis, structural analysis, comprehension, and oral reading, as well as a special selection of activities in the area of survival reading skills that will be especially useful with students at the intermediate and upper levels. The activities are sequenced according to the "Individual Pupil Checklist of Reading Skills" on pages 1-3 and the order in which the skills are generally encountered within the reading skills continuum.

Each reading skill game or activity is keyed to the Checklist of Reading Skills and provides all of the details and directions needed for its construction and effective use, including:

Name:	a distinct descriptive title
Purpose:	the specific skill/subskill that the activity is designed to reinforce
Construction:	procedures for preparing any materials needed for the activity
Players:	number of participants in the game or activity
Materials:	the materials needed by the teacher
Directions:	directions for completing the activity or playing the game

Many of the games and activities also include illustrations as a helpful reference to the construction procedures. The activities for teaching survival reading skills include complete answer keys. Many of these activities can be set up on student worksheet pages for independent use.

Sections 1 and 2 present activities to improve various phonic analysis skills such as learning to recognize letter sounds and names, consonant and vowel sounds, and vowel rules and their exceptions. Section 3 provides activities to improve the various structural analysis skills, including syllabication skills. Sections 4 and 5 contain a wide variety of activities to reinforce vocabulary, literal comprehension, and interpretive and critical reading skills. Activities in this section will help students follow directions, learn multiple meaning words, identify main ideas, draw logical conclusions, and read critically.

Section 6 provides activities to correct common problems that students encounter with oral reading, a skill that has been deemphasized in past years but has been rediscovered as an area of need in today's classroom. The activities are designed to help overcome problems such as "running over punctuation marks," poor phrasing, and poor expression.

Section 7 contains activities to build survival reading skills. Survival reading is another name for reading skills that are related to adult society, such as the ability to read and complete various forms, to interpret product information, to follow directions, and to locate and use references. The activities in this section will help students in the intermediate and the upper grades learn to read and interpret the materials they encounter in everyday situations. They will make some students realize—perhaps for the very first time—that reading is a tool that enables them to function successfully in the everyday world.

While all of the activities in this handbook will be useful in your reading improvement program, they will be of particular value when used with the informal diagnostic aids in *Informal Tests for Diagnosing Specific Reading Problems*, a separately printed handbook available from the publisher. This book provides a complete series of ready-to-use informal inventories for diagnosing each item on the "Individual Pupil Checklist of Reading Skills." These quick, reproducible diagnostic aids will help you identify and match each student's specific reading skill needs with the appropriate corrective or remedial activities.

I hope that the diversity of games, activities, and exercises presented on the following pages will help you to better meet the particular reading skill needs of all your students.

Stephen A. Pavlak

TO THE TEACHER

The following pages present a simple recordkeeping aid and an activity key to help you track each student's reading progress and match his or her needs with appropriate corrective or remedial activities.

Individual Pupil Checklist of Reading Skills

Checklists are helpful in tabulating the patterns of problems that are characteristic of disabled readers. The "Individual Pupil Checklist of Reading Skills" (pages 1-3), which specifically identifies areas of reading weakness, should be used when you are attempting to identify and remediate areas of specific reading deficiencies. It should be completed after you have administered standardized tests and informal inventories such as those presented in *Informal Tests for Diagnosing Specific Reading Problems,* available from the publisher. Because of its extensive listing of problem areas, the Checklist should prove to be an invaluable diagnostic instrument.

The Individual Pupil Checklist is designed to aid you in recording diagnosed areas of reading deficiency. In order for it to be of continuing value, you will need to reevaluate the pupil's needs and update the list frequently. The Checklist contains four error categories which are divided into appropriate skill areas:

1. Word Recognition Skills
   a. Phonetic Analysis
   b. Structural Analysis

2. Comprehension Skills
   a. Vocabulary
   b. Literal Comprehension
   c. Interpretive Comprehension
   d. Critical Reading

3. Oral Reading Skills

4. Survival Reading Skills

As you know from your own teaching experience, these four areas are of major importance

To complete and use the Checklist, place a check mark beside the skills that are known, leave the weak skills blank, and place an "X" in the blank beside the skills that have not been assessed. As the child improves in the weak skill areas and/ or the unassessed skills are evaluated, the appropriate recordkeeping marks are placed in the blanks.

Reading deficiencies identified on the Checklist are the areas you will remediate The remediation activities contained in Sections 1 through 7 of this book are keyed to the skill areas on the "Individual Pupil Checklist of Reading Skills." The Checklist as presented here is designed to be completed for each student in your classroom.

Individual Pupil Checklist of Reading Skills Activity Key

For your convenience, a special Activity Key is provided on pages 4-6. The Activity Key gives you the numbers of the activities included in this book for correcting or remediating each skill listed on the "Individual Pupil Checklist of Reading Skills." By using the Checklist and the remediation activities, you can quickly plan interesting and effective lessons to meet the particular reading needs of each student.

ACKNOWLEDGMENTS

I am indebted to my wife Patricia for her encouragement, advice, and editorial skill. Without her help, this book would not have been possible. I would also like to acknowledge the support and inspiration of my parents and my children, Stephen and Nancy

CONTENTS

Section 1

ACTIVITIES TO IMPROVE LETTER
AND LETTER SOUND RECOGNITION

Letter Sound Recognition Activities — 17

Section 2

ACTIVITIES TO IMPROVE
CONSONANT AND VOWEL RECOGNITION

Consonant Recognition Activities — 28

Vowel Recognition Activities – 48

To provide practice in recognizing CVC, CVCe, CVVC and CV vowel rules when applied

To provide practice in identifying words which contain an "o" followed by "ld" or "lt," and "a" followed by "1," "11," "w," or "u" and an "i" followed by "nd," "gh," or "ld"

To provide practice in identifying words which contain a vowel followed by an "r"

To provide practice in identifying "y" as a vowel

Section 3

ACTIVITIES TO IMPROVE STRUCTURAL ANALYSIS AND SYLLABICATION

Structural Analysis Activities – 66

To provide practice in recognizing small words in compound words

To provide practice in identifying words with inflectional endings

To provide practice in recognizing the root word from the suffix, prefix, or both affixes

To provide practice in identifying contractions

To provide practice in using possessives in context

Section 4

ACTIVITIES TO IMPROVE VOCABULARY AND LITERAL COMPREHENSION

Literal Comprehension Activities That Develop Understanding – 102

Section 5

ACTIVITIES TO IMPROVE INTERPRETIVE COMPREHENSION AND CRITICAL READING

Activities That Improve Interpretive Reading Skills – 114

Activities That Improve Critical Reading Skills – 134

Section 6

ACTIVITIES TO IMPROVE ORAL READING SKILLS

Oral Reading Activities – 140

To provide practice in using appropriate voice intonation, pitch, and stress in reading aloud

To use appropriate voice intonation, pitch, and stress to give meaning to material read aloud

To provide practice in recognizing and responding to simple punctuation marks

To provide practice in recognizing how commas affect meaning

To provide practice in reading with correct phrasing

To provide practice with phrasing and interpreting meaning

To provide practice in reading aloud with clear and distinct enunciation and appropriate expression

To provide practice in reading with an appropriate eye-voice span

Section 7

ACTIVITIES TO IMPROVE SURVIVAL READING SKILLS

Activities for Interpreting and Completing Forms – 152

To provide practice in interpreting information contained in a magazine subscription

To provide practice in interpreting information contained in a record club subscription

Activities for Interpreting Product Information – 156

To provide practice in interpreting information found on a product label

Activities for Following Directions – 167

To provide practice in reading and interpreting information found in the telephone directory

To provide practice in reading and interpreting information found in the classified telephone directory

To provide practice in following and interpreting directions found in a first aid manual

To provide practice in reading and interpreting information found on a fire extinguisher

To provide practice in reading and interpreting directions for laundering found on garment labels

To provide practice in reading and interpreting directions found in a recipe

To provide practice in reading and interpreting directions found on a frozen food package

To provide practice in reading and interpreting directions for assembling a model car

Activities for Locating and Using References – 178

To provide practice in using information found in a table of contents

To provide practice in identifying author, title, and subject cards in a card catalog

To provide practice in interpreting information found on a card in the card catalog

To provide practice in using information found in a dictionary

To provide practice in learning how to find a word in the dictionary

To provide practice in using information found in an index

To provide practice in finding information in an encyclopedia

To provide practice in interpreting information found in the *Readers' Guide to Periodical Literature*

To provide practice in interpreting information found on maps

Individual Pupil Checklist of Reading Skills

Name: _____ Grade: ____ Teacher: _____

DIRECTIONS: Place a ✔ beside each skill the child knows, leave the space blank if the child does not know the skill, and place an X beside each skill that has not been assessed.

I. Word Recognition Skills

   A. Letter Recognition
      1. Recognizes upper case letters   _____
      2. Recognizes lower case letters   _____
      3. Reverses letters   _____
      4. Inverts letters   _____
      5. Recognizes letters in the initial position   _____
      6. Recognizes letters in the medial position   _____
      7. Recognizes letters in the final position   _____
   B. Letter Sound Recognition
      1. Identifies rhymes in words   _____
      2. Identifies word family rhymes   _____
      3. Recognizes and names consonant sounds   _____
      4. Recognizes and names vowel sounds   _____
   C. Consonant Recognition
      1. Recognizes initial consonants   _____
      2. Recognizes final consonants   _____
      3. Recognizes initial two-letter blends   _____
      4. Recognizes initial three-letter blends   _____
      5. Recognizes final consonant blends   _____
      6. Recognizes initial consonant digraphs   _____
      7. Recognizes final consonant digraphs   _____
      8. Recognizes "y" as a consonant   _____
      9. Recognizes consonant irregularities
         a. Two sounds of **c**   _____
         b. Two sounds of **g**   _____
         c. **s** as **s, z,** and **sh**   _____
   D. Vowel Recognition
      1. Recognizes long vowel sounds   _____
      2. Recognizes short vowel sounds   _____
      3. Recognizes schwa sounds   _____
      4. Recognizes vowel digraphs   _____
      5. Recognizes vowel diphthongs   _____
      6. Understands vowel rules
         a. CVC   _____
         b. CVCe   _____
         c. CVVC   _____
         d. CV   _____

7. Understands vowel rule exceptions
   a. **o** followed by **ld** and **lt** _____
   b. **a** followed by **l, ll, w,** and **u** _____
   c. **i** followed by **nd, gh,** and **ld** _____
   d. vowel followed by **r** _____
   e. **y** as a vowel _____
E. Word Analysis (Structural Analysis)
   1. Can identify compound words _____
   2. Can identify inflectional endings _____
   3. Can identify root words _____
   4. Can identify contractions _____
   5. Can identify possessives _____
   6. Can identify plurals
      a. **s** _____
      b. **es** _____
      c. **ies** _____
      d. **ves** _____
      e. **y** endings _____
F. Syllabication (Structural Analysis)
   1. Can divide words into syllables
      a. one-syllable words _____
      b. two-syllable words _____
      c. three-syllable words _____
      d. four-syllable words _____
      e. five- and six-syllable words _____
   2. Can apply syllabication rules
      a. VCV _____
      b. VCCV _____
      c. Cle _____
      d. single vowel as a syllable _____
      e. consonant blends and digraphs _____
      f. prefixes and suffixes _____

II. Comprehension Skills

   A. Vocabulary
      1. Understands words in isolation _____
      2. Understands multiple meaning words in context _____
      3. Understands technical words in context _____
   B. Literal Comprehension
      1 Recalls facts read _____
      2. Follows directions read _____
      3. Sequences ideas read _____
      4. Selects important details _____
   C. Interpretive Reading Skills
      1. Can identify main ideas not explicitly stated _____
      2. Can draw logical conclusions _____
      3. Can predict logical outcomes _____
      4. Can interpret key concepts about story characters _____
      5. Can associate the text with the correct picture _____

2

6. Can follow plot sequence ____

7. Can classify information ____

8. Can determine cause-and-effect relationships ____

9. Can summarize material read ____

D. Critical Reading Skills

    1. Can identify and understand figures of speech (similes, metaphors, personification, etc.) ____

    2. Can detect and interpret propaganda techniques (testimonials, glittering generalities, bandwagon, etc.) ____

III. Oral Reading Skills

Before completing the items in this section, administer an Informal Reading Inventory or an oral reading test to the pupil. Use the diagnostic information obtained from the test to complete this section.

A. Pronounces words correctly ____

B. Uses appropriate voice intonation, pitch, and stress ____

C. Uses punctuation marks correctly during oral reading ____

D. Reads in correct phrases ____

E. Reads with clear and distinct enunciation and appropriate expression ____

F. Uses appropriate eye-voice span ____

IV. Survival Reading Skills

A. Can interpret and complete forms ____

B. Can interpret product information ____

C. Can follow directions ____

D. Can locate and use references

    1. Can use the table of contents to locate information ____

    2. Can interpret information found in the card catalog ____

    3. Can use information found in a dictionary ____

    4. Can utilize information found in an index ____

    5. Can find information in an encyclopedia ____

    6. Can interpret information found in the *Readers' Guide to Periodical Literature* ____

    7. Can interpret information found on a map ____

Individual Pupil Checklist of Reading Skills
Activity Key

The numbers in parentheses beside each skill indicate the activities that can be used to remediate the skill deficiency.

I. Word Recognition Skills
  A. Letter Recognition
    1. Recognizes upper case letters (1, 2, 3, 6)
    2. Recognizes lower case letters (4, 5, 6)
    3. Reverses letters (7, 8, 9)
    4. Inverts letters (10, 11, 12)
    5. Recognizes letters in the initial position (13, 14, 15)
    6. Recognizes letters in the medial position (16, 17, 18)
    7. Recognizes letters in the final position (19, 20, 21)
  B. Letter Sound Recognition
    1. Identifies rhymes in words (22, 23, 24, 25, 26)
    2. Identifies word family rhymes (27, 28, 29, 30, 31)
    3. Recognizes and names consonant sounds (32, 33, 34, 35, 36)
    4. Recognizes and names vowel sounds (37, 38, 39, 40, 41)
  C. Consonant Recognition
    1. Recognizes initial consonants (42, 43, 44)
    2. Recognizes final consonants (45, 46, 47)
    3. Recognizes initial two-letter blends (48, 49, 50)
    4. Recognizes initial three-letter blends (48, 49, 50)
    5. Recognizes final consonant blends (51, 52, 53)
    6. Recognizes initial consonant digraphs (54, 55, 56)
    7. Recognizes final consonant digraphs (57, 58, 59)
    8. Recognizes "y" as a consonant (60, 61)
    9. Recognizes consonant irregularities
      a. Two sounds of **c** (62, 63)
      b. Two sounds of **g** (64, 65)
      c. **s** as **s, z,** and **sh** (66, 67)
  D. Vowel Recognition
    1. Recognizes long vowel sounds (68, 69, 70, 71, 72, 73)
    2. Recognizes short vowel sounds (68, 69, 70, 71, 72, 73)
    3. Recognizes schwa sounds (74, 75)
    4. Recognizes vowel digraphs (76, 77, 78)
    5. Recognizes vowel diphthongs (79, 80, 81)
    6. Understands vowel rules
      a. CVC (82, 83, 84, 85, 86)
      b. CVCe (82, 83, 84, 85, 86)
      c. CVVC (82, 83, 84, 85, 86)
      d. CV (82, 83, 84, 85, 86)

      7. Understands vowel rule exceptions
        a. **o** followed by **ld** and **lt** (87, 88, 89)
        b. **a** followed by **l, ll, w,** and **u** (87, 88, 89)
        c. **i** followed by **nd, gh,** and **ld** (87, 88, 89)
        d. vowel followed by **r** (90, 91)
        e. **y** as a vowel (92, 93)
    E. Word Analysis (Structural Analysis)
      1. Can identify compound words (94, 95, 96)
      2. Can identify inflectional endings (97, 98, 99)
      3. Can identify root words (100, 101, 102)
      4. Can identify contractions (103, 104, 105)
      5. Can identify possessives (106, 107, 108)
      6. Can identify plurals
        a. **s** (109, 110, 111)
        b. **es** (109, 110, 111)
        c. **ies** (109, 110, 111)
        d. **ves** (109, 110, 111)
        e. **y** endings (109, 110, 111)
    F. Syllabication (Structural Analysis)
      1. Can divide words into syllables
        a. one-syllable words (112, 113, 114, 115, 116)
        b. two-syllable words (112, 113, 114, 115, 116)
        c. three-syllable words (112, 113, 114, 115, 116)
        d. four-syllable words (112, 113, 114, 115, 116)
        e. five- and six-syllable words (112, 113, 114, 115, 116)
      2. Can apply syllabication rules
        a. VCV (117, 118, 119)
        b. VCCV (117, 118, 119)
        c. Cle (117, 118, 119)
        d. single vowel as a syllable (120, 121, 122)
        e. consonant blends and digraphs (123, 124, 125)
        f. prefixes and suffixes (126, 127, 128)
II. Comprehension Skills
    A. Vocabulary
      1. Understands words in isolation (129, 130, 131, 132)
      2. Understands multiple meaning words in context (133, 134, 135, 136)
      3. Understands technical words in context (137, 138, 139, 140)
    B. Literal Comprehension
      1. Recalls facts read (141, 142, 143, 144)
      2. Follows directions read (145, 146, 147, 148)
      3. Sequences ideas read (149, 150, 151, 152)
      4. Selects important details (153, 154, 155)
    C. Interpretive Reading Skills
      1. Can identify main ideas not explicitly stated (156, 157, 158)
      2. Can draw logical conclusions (159, 160, 161)

        3. Can predict logical outcomes (162, 163, 164)

        4. Can interpret key concepts about story characters (165, 166, 167)

        5. Can associate the text with the correct picture (168, 169, 170)

        6. Can follow plot sequence (171, 172, 173)

        7. Can classify information (174, 175, 176)

        8. Can determine cause-and-effect relationships (177, 178, 179)

        9. Can summarize material read (180, 181, 182)

    D. Critical Reading Skills

        1. Can identify and understand figures of speech (similes, metaphors, personification, etc.) (183, 184, 185)

        2. Can detect and interpret propaganda techniques (testimonials, glittering generalities, bandwagon, etc.) (186, 187, 188)

III. Oral Reading Skills

    A. Pronounces words correctly (189, 190, 191)

    B. Uses appropriate voice intonation, pitch, and stress (192, 193, 194)

    C. Uses punctuation marks correctly during oral reading (195, 196, 197)

    D. Reads in correct phrases (198, 199, 200)

    E. Reads with clear and distinct enunciation and appropriate expression (201, 202, 203)

    F. Uses appropriate eye-voice span (204, 205, 206)

IV. Survival Reading Skills

    A. Can interpret and complete forms (207, 208)

    B. Can interpret product information (209, 210, 211, 212, 213, 214, 215)

    C. Can follow directions (216, 217, 218, 219, 220, 221, 222, 223, 224)

    D. Can locate and use references

        1. Can use the table of contents to locate information (225)

        2. Can interpret information found in the card catalog (226, 227)

        3. Can use information found in a dictionary (228, 229)

        4. Can utilize information found in an index (230, 231)

        5. Can find information in an encyclopedia (232)

        6. Can interpret information found in the *Readers' Guide to Periodical Literature* (233)

        7. Can interpret information found on a map (234)

ACTIVITIES TO IMPROVE LETTER AND LETTER SOUND RECOGNITION

LETTER RECOGNITION ACTIVITIES

The following activities teach the pupil to recognize upper and lower case letters in the initial, medial, and final positions, to match upper and lower case letters, and to cope with the tendency to reverse or invert letters.

1: Alphabet Feet

Purpose: To provide practice in recognizing upper case letters.

Construction: Write various upper case letters on feet made from posterboard. Place the feet on the floor in a line to represent the alphabet path.

Players: Two or more

Materials: Posterboard, marker, scissors, masking tape

Directions: The players take turns trying to follow the path by saying the name of the upper case letter on each foot before stepping on it. If a player misses a letter, he must start back at the beginning. Anyone who successfully follows the path receives one point. The player with the most points at the end of the game wins. The feet can be replaced by other letter feet or the order can be changed.

2: Superman

Purpose: To provide practice in recognizing upper case letters.

Construction: Use index cards to make two sets of upper case letter cards. Write a letter on each card. On one card, paste a picture of Superman.

Players: Two or more

Materials: Index cards (3″ × 5″), marker, picture of Superman

Directions: Each player is dealt an even number of cards. The players take turns drawing a card from the player to the right. When a player gets a match, he must lay it down. The first player to get rid of all his cards except the Superman card is the winner.

3: Letter Detective

Purpose: To provide practice in recognizing upper case letters.

Construction: Trace and cut out upper case letters of the alphabet on sandpaper. Glue the letters to separate sheets of oaktag. One letter should be glued to one piece of oaktag.

Players: One or more

Materials: Sandpaper, oaktag, blindfolds, scissors, glue

Directions: Each player is given those upper case letters of the alphabet which he does not know (no more than five letters at a time). He is allowed to study the pile of letters, and then he is blindfolded. While blindfolded, he is asked to trace the letters and tell what they are. For each letter correctly identified, the player receives one point. When more than one player is playing, the first player to identify the letter is awarded the point. The player with the most points is the winner.

4: Letter Twins

Purpose: To provide practice in recognizing lower case letters.

Construction: Write various lower case letters on index cards. There should be two cards of each letter. Place the cards face down on a table. Use five or six sets of cards at a time.

Players: Two or more

Materials: Index cards (3″ × 5″), marker

Directions: The players take turns turning over two cards at a time to see if they can get a match. If they get a match, they get to keep the cards. The game continues until all the cards are gone. The player with the most cards at the end of the game is the winner.

5: Bingo Letters

Purpose: To provide practice in recognizing lower case letters.

Construction: Make bingo cards from posterboard (use 5″ × 6″ pieces). Divide the cards into five columns and five rows. Write a lower case letter in each square except for the center square which is identified as a "Free Space." Write lower case letters on 2″ × 2″ squares and place them in a small paper bag.

Players: Two or small groups

Materials: Posterboard, marker, scissors, construction paper, small paper bag, markers for bingo cards (buttons, beans, etc.)

Directions: Pick a letter from the paper bag and call it out. The players look to see if that letter is on their cards and place a marker on it. The first player to get five in a row across, down, or diagonally is the winner.

6: Letter Match

Purpose: To provide practice in matching upper and lower case letters.

Construction: Cut a piece of oaktag into a circle, or use cardboard circles similar to those which are used with pizzas and glue the oaktag to it. Print upper case letters in random order around the outer edge of the circle. Cut another smaller piece of oaktag which will fit in the middle of the larger one and print lower case letters around its outer edge. Fasten the two circles in the middle with a brass fastener. Example:

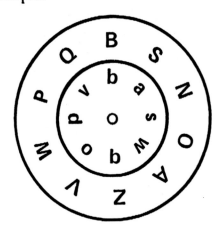

Players: One

Materials: Oaktag sheets, marker, brass fastener, (optional: large cardboard circle)

Directions: Say a letter and instruct the child to turn the inner circle to match the appropriate outer letter. The student may also use the device for independent work.

7: Sandy Letter

Purpose: To correct the reversal of letters.

Construction: Place some sand in a large shoe box or gift box.

Players: One

Materials: Sand, shoe box or gift box

Directions: Call out a letter and instruct the player to print the letter in the sand with his finger. Students who are having difficulty printing the letter from memory may have to copy from a printed list of letters and/or have individual help.

8: Clay Letter

Purpose: To correct the reversal of letters.

Construction: Give each child a stick of modeling clay to use in forming the letters.

Players: One or small group

Materials: Modeling clay, chalk

Directions: On the chalkboard print a letter that is commonly reversed. Each child who is having trouble with that letter will be given a stick of modeling clay. The child will form the letter out of clay and then trace over it several times with his finger. A way of adding interest to the activity is to have the children compete to see who will be the first to complete the letter.

9: Trace a Letter

Purpose: To correct the reversal of letters

Construction: At the top of a sheet of paper, print letters that the student reverses. Write the incomplete letters on lines below the printed letters. Example:

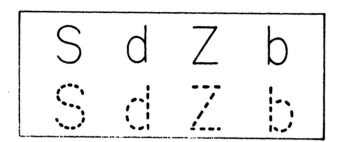

Players: One

Materials: Paper, marker

Directions: To have the child learn which letter is printed, have him trace over the incomplete letter. Incomplete letters may be traced on the paper as many times as necessary. When the child is able to trace over the letters without making an error, he can then print his own letter below the one he has traced. Letters that are successfully printed should then be cut out and placed in an envelope. The letters in the envelope will provide a record of letters learned.

10: Letter Magic

Purpose: To correct inversion of letters.

Construction: Print letters that are commonly inverted on a sheet of paper, using a glue stick.

Players: One

Materials: Glue stick, paper, sparkles, marker

Directions: Have the child sprinkle sparkles over the glue to discover the invisible letter. After the sparkles have adhered to the glue and dried, have the child trace over the letter with his finger. When he is able to freely trace the letter, let him practice printing it under the sparkle letter. He should repeat tracing the sparkle letter if he encounters any difficulty.

11: Letter Pattern

Purpose: To correct inversion of letters.

Construction: Using letters that are commonly inverted, cut out oaktag letters and sandpaper letters of the same size (2″ or 3″). Cut out two sets of each letter—one oaktag, one sandpaper. Paste or fasten the oaktag letters to separate squares of oaktag, approximately 4″ squares.

Players: One

Materials: Oaktag, sandpaper, colored markers, paper

Directions: Have the child color the oaktag letters with markers. Place the colored oaktag letter squares and the sandpaper letters on the desk in front of the child and instruct him to match the sandpaper letters to the appropriate colored oaktag letters. Matched letters should be placed one on top of the other. He then traces the sandpaper letter several times until he can do this with a smooth motion. He should then print the letter with marker on a separate sheet of paper as he looks at the sandpaper letter.

12: Letter Proof

Purpose: To correct inversion of letters.

Construction: On a sheet of paper write various letters with the inverted forms beside them. Leave space for the student to practice printing the letter.

Players: One

Materials: Paper, marker

Directions: The player will circle the correct letter form and then practice printing it in the space provided.

13: Picture Paste-Up

Purpose: To provide practice in recognizing letters in the initial position.

Construction: Print various letters at the top and middle of a sheet of oaktag. Arrange the letters so that there is space below each one to paste a picture.

Players: One

Materials: Magazines with pictures, scissors, glue stick, marker, oaktag sheets

Directions: Have the student look through the magazines and cut out pictures representing words that begin with the letters on the oaktag sheet. Have the student paste the picture below the correct initial letter on the oaktag sheet.

14: Picture-Word Match

Purpose: To provide practice in recognizing letters in the initial position.

Construction: Write various words in a column on a paper. In another column, paste pictures representing words that have the same initial letters as the various words in the first column. Mix the order of the pictures in the second column so that they differ from the order of the initial letters of the words in the first column.

Players: One

Materials: Paper, pen or pencil

Directions: The student will match the words in the first column with the pictures in the second column that have the same initial letter. The student will do this by drawing lines from the words in the first column to the pictures in the second column

15: Word Elimination

Purpose: To provide practice in recognizing letters in the initial position.

Construction: Write four words that have the same initial letter and one word that does not. Do this for approximately five groups of words.

Players: One

Materials: Paper, pen or pencil

Directions: The student will cross out the word in each group that does not have the same initial letter as the other words in the group. Use letters that are troublesome for the student.

16: Chickens and Eggs

Purpose: To provide practice in recognizing letters in the medial position.

Construction: Make 15 chickens and 15 eggs out of construction paper. Write a word on each chicken and a word on each egg with the same medial letters. The chickens and eggs should match one-to-one.

Players: One

Materials: Construction paper, scissors, marker

Directions: The student will match the chicken with the egg that has the same medial letter. The student will do this by putting the chickens next to the matching egg. To make the words easy to see, spread the chickens and eggs out on a large table.

17: Medial Race

Purpose: To provide practice in recognizing letters in the medial position.

Construction: Divide the outside edges of a rectangular piece of posterboard into squares. Attach troublesome medial letter words to the squares. Make a spinner out of a piece of posterboard. Example:

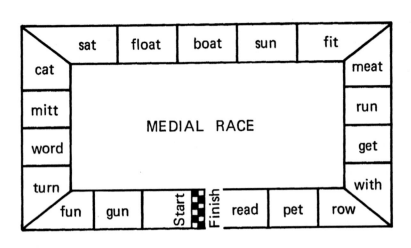

Players: Two to four

Materials: Posterboard, paper fastener, staple gun or other material useful for fastening words to track, place markers

Directions: The player spins the spinner to determine the number of spaces to move. In order to stay on the space, the player must read the word attached to the space. If he cannot read the word, he goes back to a space where he can read the word. Players take turns, and the game continues until a player crosses the finish line. Additional tracks can be made by clipping different words to the track.

18: Fish 'n Worms

Purpose: To provide practice in recognizing letters in the medial position.

Construction: On a piece of posterboard, draw an underwater scene. Cut different types of fish from construction paper, and on each fish print a word that contains a troublesome medial letter. Cut worms from brown construction paper and print a word with a medial letter on each worm. Medial letters on the fish should match those on the worms. A substitute for the construction paper worms would be pieces of yarn with cards attached to them on which the words are written.

Players: One or small group

Materials: Posterboard, construction paper, marker, scissors, small box (optional: yarn)

Directions: Place several fish on the underwater scene. In a small box, place the worms for "bait." The student takes a worm from the box, reads the word on it, and matches the medial letter to the correct fish on the underwater scene. The student "catches" the fish with a correct match and continues using the worms to match medial letters until all of the fish have been caught. If done with a small group, players take turns "fishing" and the player who catches the most fish is the winner. The game can be varied by changing the fish that are used each time.

19: Letter Bag

Purpose: To provide practice in recognizing letters in the final position.

Construction: Place various objects in a paper bag. Objects such as beads, shells, bottle caps, shoe laces, paper clips, etc., can be used.

Players: One or total group

Materials: Paper bag, various objects to place in the bag

Directions: The student reaches into the bag, selects an object and takes it out of the bag, says its name, and gives another word that ends with the same final letter. The activity is continued until all the objects have been taken from the bag.

20: Final Fish

Purpose: To provide practice in recognizing letters in the final position.

Construction: Using index cards, make two sets of playing cards. One set of cards will contain words with troublesome final letters and one set will contain pictures representing the words. On one card paste a picture of a fish.

Players: Two or more

Materials: Index cards (3″ × 5″), marker, pictures

Directions: Each player is dealt an even number of cards. The players take turns drawing a card from the player on the right. When a player matches a picture with the correct word, he must put the two cards down. The first player to get rid of all his cards is the winner. Play continues until one player is left with the "Final Fish."

21: Final Challenge

Purpose: To provide practice in recognizing letters in the final position.

Construction: Print various words on index cards. Cut 2″ squares out of oaktag and print a letter on each square using all letters of the alphabet. Make a set of letter squares for each player.

Players: Two or more

Materials: Index cards (3″ × 5″), marker, scissors, oaktag

Directions: Show a word card for two to three seconds to the players. Each player will use the letter squares to form a word that has the same final letter as the word shown. The player who is the first to form a correct word receives one point. The player with the most points at the end of the game is the winner.

LETTER SOUND RECOGNITION ACTIVITIES

The remaining activities in this section teach the pupil to hear rhymes in words, to give the sounds of initial and final consonants, to differentiate between the sounds of similar two- and three-letter blends and digraphs in the initial position, and to distinguish between the long and short sounds of vowels.

22: Rhyme or Not

Purpose: To provide practice in hearing rhymes in words.

Construction: Collect various pictures from magazines. Get two small boxes. Label one "Rhyme" and the other "Not."

Players: One

Materials: Pictures, two small boxes, marker

Directions: The player will be given two pictures. The player must decide if the pictures represent rhymes or not. If they are rhymes, they should be placed in the "Rhyme" box. If they do not rhyme, they should be placed in the "Not" box.

23: Rhyme Dash

Purpose: To provide practice in hearing rhymes in words.

Construction: Draw a 100-yard dash race on a piece of poster board. Make a starting line and a finish line. Draw a line to mark every 10 yards. Have three buttons for place markers. Write two words on each of 40 index cards. Some of the words should represent rhymes and others should not.

Players: Two or three

Materials: Posterboard, glue, pencil, crayons, marker, index cards (3″ × 5″), three buttons

Directions: The players will take turns picking a card. Each player must read the words on the card and tell if they rhyme or not. If the player is correct, he is allowed to move to the next 10-yard line. The player who reaches the finish line first wins the game.

24: Rhyme Review

Purpose: To provide practice in hearing rhymes in words.

Construction: Make a list of words that have many other rhyming words (no, sleigh, boat, flew, sea, prey, etc.)

Players: Total group

Materials: Paper, pencils, chalkboard, chalk

Directions: Say one word from the list that you have prepared and instruct the students to write as many rhyming words as they can for that word. Students may then share their answers orally with the group and compile a list on the chalkboard. Other variations would be (1) to have several students write their lists on the chalkboard and compare their answers, (2) to see which student can write the most correct rhyming words, and (3) to compile the list as a group with each student taking a turn to give a rhyming word.

25: Rhyme-a-Pillar

Purpose: To provide practice in hearing rhymes in words.

Construction: Using construction paper, cut out the head of a caterpillar or similar creature. Cut other sections for the body of the caterpillar from various colors of construction paper. Attach the head to the bulletin board and place the first section behind the head.

Players: Small group or total group

Materials: Construction paper, scissors, markers, rubber cement or masking tape

Directions: Print a word on the first section of the caterpillar on the bulletin board. Select a student who volunteers to come to the bulletin board. He will print a word that rhymes with the word on the first section on another section of the caterpillar, pronounce the word, and then attach that section to the caterpillar on the bulletin board. The class then pronounces all the sections in unison. Continue this procedure until the "Rhyme-a-Pillar" has been completed.

26: Rhyme Relay

Purpose: To provide practice with rhymes in words.

Construction: Paste pictures that have been cut out or draw pictures on index cards. Print words on index cards that will rhyme with the pictures.

Players: Three small groups

Materials: Index cards (3″ × 5″), marker, pictures, chalkboard, chalk

Directions: Divide the group of children into three teams. Each team will line up six feet from the front chalkboard. Rhyming words are placed on a desk beside the leader of each team, and pictures that rhyme with the words are placed on the front chalkboard. Each child on the team will select a word from the pile and go to the board to select a picture which rhymes with that word. To be awarded a point for his team, the child must then write a third rhyming word on the board. The first team to have all its players write appropriate rhyming words on the board is the winner. A variation of the relay game is to require the children to write more than one rhyming word on the board.

27: The Lion or the Clown

Purpose: To provide practice in recognizing word family rhymes.

Construction: Write three words on each of 20 index cards. Some of the words should represent word family rhymes (such as look, book, cook) and others should not rhyme. Using two plastic milk cartons, label one "Rhymes" and the other "Not Rhymes." Using construction paper and marker, make the carton that is labeled "Rhymes" look like a lion and the carton labeled "Not Rhymes" look like a clown.

Players: One

Materials: Index cards (3″ × 5″), construction paper, marker, two plastic milk cartons

Directions: The player will read the three words on each index card. The player must decide whether or not the words represent a word family rhyme. If the words rhyme, the index card is to be placed in the Lion carton. If the words do not rhyme, the player places the index card in the Clown carton.

28: Doggie Dinner

Purpose: To provide practice in recognizing word family rhymes.

Construction: Cut out pictures of various breeds of dogs (collies, springers, poodles, etc.) and mount them on stiff paper. Under each picture print a word family name (-ate, -ook, -at, etc.). Cut out bones from stiff paper and print initial sounds on them. At the top of each bone punch a hole. Under the dog picture and to the left of the word family name, attach a hook or paste on a pocket large enough to hold the bones.

Players: One (or small group divided into teams)

Materials: Pictures of dogs, stiff paper, metal hooks, marker, scissors, paper
punch

Directions: A sheet with one of the dog pictures on it is given to each team of
students. The bones with the various initial sounds are placed in piles.
The object of the game is to feed the dog as many bones as possible
(rhyming words made by adding the initial sound on the bone to the
word family name printed beneath the dog picture). When a word is
formed, the bone containing the initial sound is hung on the hook or
placed in the pocket. The team that "feeds the dog" the most correct
bones is the winner. This activity is also appropriate for use with an
individual student rather than a team.

29: Word Family Match

Purpose: To provide practice in recognizing word family rhymes.

Construction: Pick a word family ending (-ook, -it, -at, etc.) and write it on the
chalkboard. Distribute paper to each player in the group.

Players: Large group

Materials: Chalkboard, chalk, paper, pencils

Directions: The players will write the word family ending on their papers. They
will then try to make as many words as possible by adding letters or
letter combinations to the front of the word family ending. The words
that are formed may not be nonsense words. The player with the most
correct words at the end of 30 seconds wins the game. The winner
must read his list of words to the class. Use the same procedure with
other word family endings. In the higher grades, the player could be
required to use his words in a sentence. The time limit would be
adjusted to incorporate this activity.

30: Do You Know?

Purpose: To provide practice in recognizing word family rhymes.

Construction: Write two words on each of 40 index cards. Some of the words
should represent word family rhymes and the others should not.
Place the cards face down on a table.

Players: Two or three

Materials: Index cards (3″ × 5″), marker, a die

Directions: The players will roll a die to determine who goes first, second and
third. The players will take turns picking a card from the pile, reading
the two words on it, and telling whether or not the words rhyme. If the

words rhyme, the player must say a third word which will also rhyme. If the player is correct, he keeps the card. If not, the card should be placed on the bottom of the pile. The player with the most cards at the end of the game is the winner.

31: Shake and Say

Purpose: To provide practice in recognizing word family rhymes.

Construction: Write 12 word-family words (sat, sit, look, etc.) on self-adhesive labels. Cut each of the labels small enough to fit into the bottom of an egg carton pocket. Place the labels inside the egg carton (one word per pocket).

Players: One or two

Materials: One egg carton, self-adhesive labels, bingo marker or button

Directions: Place a bingo marker or button inside the egg carton and close the lid. Instruct the player to shake the carton, open it, read the word that is under the marker, and give a word that rhymes. The activity can be expanded by placing two words in the pocket of the egg carton and asking the player to say two additional rhyming words.

32: Racing Consonants

Purpose: To provide practice in giving the sounds of initial or final consonants.

Construction: Draw a circular race track on a large piece of posterboard. Divide the track into numerous sections and print a word with a consonant in the initial or final position in each section. Make a starting line and a finish line. Use small toy cars as place holders.

Players: Two or three

Materials: Posterboard, marker, crayons, a die, three small toy cars

Directions: The players take turns rolling the die and moving that many spaces on the race track. Wherever he lands, the player must say the word and give the sound of the initial or final consonant. If the player is correct, he stays on that space. If he misses, he must move back one space, say the word on that space, and give the sound of the initial or final consonant. If the player is incorrect again, he loses his turn and stays on that space. The first car to cross the finish line is the winner of the "Racing Consonants."

33: Letter Cat

Purpose: To provide practice in giving the sounds of initial or final consonants.

Construction: On index cards print various words with consonants in the initial or final position. Place the cards in a paper bag that has been made to look like a cat's face.

Players: One

Materials: Index cards (3″ × 5″), paper bag, marker

Directions: The player will reach into the bag and pull out a card. The player must say the word, give the sound of the initial or final consonant, and say a word of his own that begins or ends with the same consonant sound.

34: Sounds of Consonants

Purpose: To provide practice in differentiating the sounds of similar two- and three-letter blends and digraphs in the initial position.

Construction: On a sheet of paper, glue pictures in groups of four. Three of the pictures should represent words that have the same initial blend or digraph sound, and one should be different from the other three.

Players: One or small group

Materials: Paper, pictures, glue, pencil

Directions: The player looks at the pictures and puts an X on the picture that does not have the same initial blend or digraph sound as the other three. The activity can also be used with a small group by having the children compete to see who can be first to identify the incorrect picture.

35: Triple Play

Purpose: To provide practice in differentiating the sounds of similar two- and three-letter blends and digraphs in the initial position.

Construction: On each of 25 index cards, print three words. Some sets of words should have the same initial blend or digraph sounds and others should not.

Players: Two equal groups

Materials: Index cards (3″ × 5″), marker

Directions: The groups will take turns sending a player to the front of the room. Read three words from a card to the player whose turn it is. The player must decide if the words have the same initial blend or digraph sound. If the player is correct, his team receives one point. The team with the most points at the end of the game wins.

36: Sound Directions

Purpose: To provide practice in differentiating the sounds of similar two- and three-letter blends and digraphs in the initial position.

Construction: On each of 10 to 15 index cards, print a set of directions. For example, "Circle the picture on your answer sheet that has the same initial blend sound as the word *blue*" and "Make an X over the picture on your answer sheet that has the same initial digraph sound as the word *shop*." To make an answer sheet, take a sheet of paper and glue on pictures that provide answers to correspond to the directions on the cards.

Players: One

Materials: Paper, pictures, pencil, index cards (3″ × 5″), glue

Directions: In the early grades, read aloud the directions on the card and have the student correctly identify the appropriate picture on his answer sheet. Students who are able to read should be allowed to read the directions for themselves.

37: Short and Long Vowel Box

Purpose: To provide practice in distinguishing between short and long sounds of vowels.

Construction: Label each of ten shoe boxes with each of the short and long vowels. On index cards, print various words that contain the short and long vowel sounds. To add interest, the shoe boxes should be decorated with Con-Tact paper.

Players: One

Materials: Index cards (3″ × 5″), marker, ten shoe boxes, Con-Tact paper

Directions: The player will choose a card, read the word on the card, and place it in the correct box according to the short or long vowel sound. The activity can also be done with picture cards instead of word cards.

38: Vowel Baskets

Purpose: To provide practice in distinguishing between short and long sounds of vowels.

Construction: Draw ten flower baskets on a large piece of posterboard. Place a picture hook on each basket and mark the top of the basket with each of the long and short vowels. Make 50 flowers out of construction paper and write words on them which contain each of the long and short vowel sounds (5 flowers for each vowel sound). Punch a hole in the top of each flower. Make a score card for each player.

Players: Small group

Materials: Posterboard, picture hooks, marker, construction paper, scissors, crayons, pencils

Directions: The player will select one flower, read the word on it, decide on the vowel sound, and hang the flower on the appropriately labeled basket. The player will receive one point on his score card for each flower correctly matched to a basket. If the player's match is incorrect, the flower is placed on the bottom of the pile. The next player then repeats this process and play continues until all of the flowers have been matched. The player with the most points is the winner. At the conclusion of the game, the players may read aloud each group of correctly matched words as a review of the vowel sounds.

39: Short-Long Concentration

Purpose: To provide practice in distinguishing between short and long sounds of vowels.

Construction: Attach 20 hooks to a large piece of posterboard or heavy cardboard (4 rows across and 5 rows down). Space should be left so that index cards can be hung from each hook. Print the numbers 1 through 20 on 20 index cards. Select ten words to represent short and long vowel sounds and make two index cards for each word. Punch holes in each of the index cards. Arrange the word cards on the playing board and then cover the word cards with the number cards in order from 1 to 20. The playing board should resemble a "Concentration" game board.

Players: Two or more

Materials: Posterboard or heavy cardboard, picture hooks, marker, index cards (3″ × 5″), paper punch

Directions: The player calls a number and you remove the number card from the hook to reveal the word behind it. The player must then say the word that is uncovered and identify the vowel sounds in the word. If he is correct, he calls out another number in an attempt to uncover the second card for that same word. If he is successful in locating the second card, he keeps both numbers. If he is unsuccessful, both numbers are returned to the playing board. Players must concentrate to remember where words are located. Play continues until all number cards have been removed from the playing board The player with the most number cards is the winner

40: Vowel-Go-Round

Purpose: To provide practice in distinguishing between short and long sounds of vowels.

Construction: Using posterboard, cut out a horselike animal and two circles. One small circle will be attached behind the animal's head, and the larger circle will be attached behind his body. Cut a rectangular opening in the jaw and attach the small circle so that the vowel letters and their diacritical markings can be seen through the opening. Cut a rectangular opening in the animal's body and attach the larger circle so that a word can be seen through it.

Illustration:

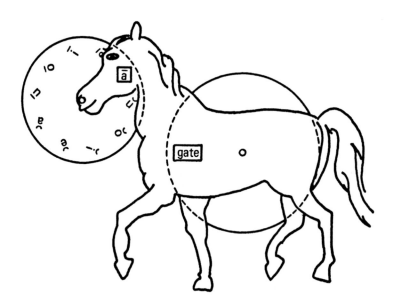

Simple word list for the larger circle:

happy	sock
gate	glue
heat	met
bat	kite

Players: One

Materials: Posterboard, fabric scraps of various kinds to decorate the animal, paper fasteners, crayons, marker, scissors

Directions: Move the larger wheel to locate a word in the window. The player will match the word with its corresponding vowel sound by rotating the wheel on the animal's head until the correct vowel sound appears. The larger wheel can be changed so that many words can be reviewed. If the answers are written on the back of the larger wheel, the activity can be self-checking.

41: Tic-Tac-Vowel

Purpose: To provide practice in distinguishing between short and long sounds of vowels.

Construction: Make a tic-tac-toe playing board 8″ × 8″ in size out of posterboard. Make numerous 2″ × 2″ cards out of posterboard or index cards. Print X's on the front side of half of the cards and print O's on the front side of the remainder. On the other side of the cards print words containing short or long vowel sounds (such as say, her, fat, toy, ice, blue, etc.).

Players: Two

Materials: Posterboard, index cards, marker

Directions: Give one player the X cards and the other palyer the O cards. The player with the X cards turns over the one card and pronounces the word. If he is correct, he places his X card on a space of the Tic-Tac-Vowel playing board. The player with the O cards then turns over one of his cards and pronounces the word. If he is correct, he places his O card on a space of the Tic-Tac-Vowel playing board. The first player to get Tic-Tac-Vowel wins (same symbols horizontally, vertically, or diagonally).

Section 2

ACTIVITIES TO IMPROVE CONSONANT AND VOWEL RECOGNITION

CONSONANT RECOGNITION ACTIVITIES

The following activities teach the pupil to identify initial and final consonants, initial two- and three-letter blends, final consonant blends, initial and final consonant digraphs, "y" as a consonant, and the special sounds of the letters "c," "g," and "s."

42: Consonant Race

Purpose: To provide practice in identifying initial consonants.

Construction: Use a large sheet of oaktag and attach small oaktag circles to it with tape or other adhesive material. Two lines of circles should be placed in a zigzag pattern across the sheet so that there are an equal number of circles in each line. Using the consonants that are to be taught, print one consonant on the front of each circle. Using cloth material, cut two rectangular ribbons. Attach the ribbons to the oaktag sheet so that one ribbon is near the top of the sheet and at the end of the first line of circles, and the other ribbon is near the bottom and at the end of the second line of circles. The ribbons will serve as goal lines.

Example:

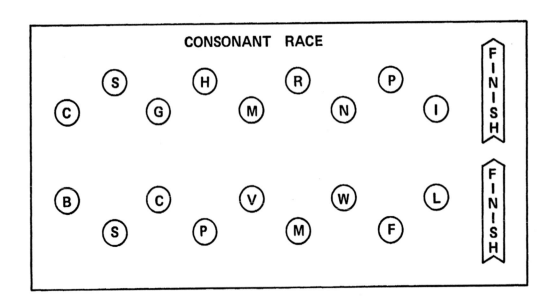

Players: Two or more

Materials: Oaktag, marker, scissors, cloth material, tape or other adhesive material

Directions: Divide the children into two teams and select appropriate team names. Tell the children that one team will win by reaching the ribbon before the other team. The first player will point to the first circle in his team's line and say a word that begins with that consonant. If he answers correctly, he may remove the circle to show that his team is moving toward the ribbon. If he answers incorrectly, he steps to the rear of the line without removing the circle. The first player on the second team then takes a turn. The teams alternate turns until one team reaches the ribbon. The game may be concluded when one team reaches the ribbon or, if additional practice with initial consonants is needed, points may be scored. For example, one point is awarded to the team as it reaches the ribbon, the consonant circles are returned to the board, and the game continues until one team reaches a previously established score such as five points.

43: Score "10"

Purpose: To provide practice in identifying initial consonants.

Construction: Have each child write numbers one to ten on a sheet of tablet paper. Each child must have a partner (buddy) for this activity.

Players: Two or more

Materials: Tablet paper, pencils

Directions: Read aloud a list of ten words beginning with the consonants that you are teaching (Sand, Coast, Doctor, etc.). The children must write the words and underline the beginning consonants. Beside each of the ten words dictated to him, the child must then write a word of his own that begins with the same consonant sound as the dictated word. After writing his own ten words, he and his buddy exchange papers and check to see if the words that were written are correct. If the child finds an incorrect word, he circles it and deducts one point from the total score of ten. The papers are then returned. Each of the players then writes ten more words on his paper. This procedure is followed for three turns (or any number of turns to be determined by the teacher). The winner of the exercise is the child who has written the most correct words. All scores are verified by the teacher. The teacher must try to match children of similar abilities in order for this activity to be of maximum usefulness.

44: Consonant Teamwork

Purpose: To provide practice in identifying initial consonants.

Construction: Using index cards, make two sets of consonant letter cards. Use all of the consonants in the alphabet or limit the activity to those consonants you are teaching. Make a list of words with initial consonants to correspond with the letter cards.

Players: Entire class or small group

Materials: Index cards (5″ × 8″), markers

Directions: Divide the group into two teams. Distribute one set of letter cards to the members of each team, each child having one card. To begin the game, call out one word from the list—for example, "Sat." Each player determines if his card has the initial consonant for "Sat" and raises his card if it does. Since two players will have an "S" card (one player on each team), the child who raises his card first will have the opportunity to earn a point for his team. To earn the point, the child who raises his "S" card first must then give the sound the consonant makes in the word. If he correctly says the sound, his team is awarded one point. If he is incorrect, the member of the opposite team with the "S" card has an opportunity to win the point. The game continues in this manner with the words on the list, and the team with the most points is the winner.

45: Consonant Cut-Ups

Purpose: To provide practice in identifying final consonants.

Construction: Use sheets of construction paper to make word-listing cards. At the top of each sheet print a consonant.

Players: One or more

Materials: Construction paper, marker, magazines, newspapers, paste, scissors

Directions: Give each child a sheet of construction paper with a consonant printed at the top. Instruct each child to look through magazines and/or newspapers to find words that end with the consonant printed on his sheet. When he finds a word, he is to cut it out and paste it on his sheet. Each child should attempt to find as many words as possible. Words that the child pastes on the sheet may then be used in further activities. A variation of the exercise would be to have the child cut out and paste pictures and then print the words that end with the consonant on his sheet.

46: Final Toss

Purpose: To provide practice in identifying final consonants.

Construction: Use a large cardboard box and cut a face in the top of the box. The holes must be cut large enough to allow a beanbag to easily pass through them. Decorate the box with Con-Tact paper or other appropriate material. Make beanbags small enough to fit through the holes in the box. On index cards, print various words that end with consonants. The number of cards will vary according to grade level of the children and the length of the game.

Example:

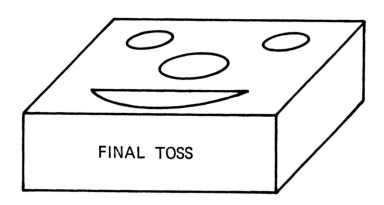

FINAL TOSS

Players: Two or more

Materials: Cardboard box, scissors, Con-Tact paper, beanbags, index cards (3″ × 5″)

Directions: Assign each of the holes in the box a numerical value—for example, the mouth is one point, the nose is two points, an eye is three points. Divide the children into two teams. Children on each team will take turns tossing two beanbags at the face. Each time a beanbag falls through one of the holes in the face, the child must choose an index card from the pile and then (1) pronounce the word on the card, (2) identify the final consonant, and (3) give the sound of the final consonant. If the child is correct, he earns the appropriate number of points. The teams alternate turns until the game is concluded. The winner is the team with the most points. A variation of the game is to have each child pronounce the word on the index card, identify the final consonant, give the sound of the final consonant, and give another word that ends with the same final consonant.

The distance of the toss is determined by the grade level of the children. Older children will stand further away from the box than will younger children.

47: Consonant Cup

Purpose: To provide practice in identifying final consonants.

Construction: Write 12 consonants on self-adhesive labels. Cut each of the labels small enough to fit into the bottom of an egg carton cup. Place the labels inside the egg carton (one consonant per cup).

Players: One or more

Materials: Egg carton, self-adhesive labels, two buttons

Directions: Each child will toss two buttons into the egg carton cups. To earn a point for each of the buttons, the child must say a word that ends with the consonant in the cup. The player receives one point for each correct word given.

48: Racing Blends

Purpose: To provide practice in identifying initial two- and three-letter blends.

Construction: Make a game board out of posterboard. Divide the game board into small sections. Laminate the game board or cover it with clear Con-Tact paper. In each small section of the game board, print (using a grease pencil) a word that contains a two-letter blend or a three-letter blend in the initial position. The game board can be any shape and contain as many words as needed.

Example of one type of gameboard:

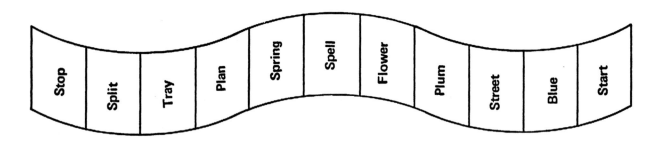

Players: Two to four

Materials: Posterboard, grease pencil, scissors, a die, place markers

Directions: Each player will take turns rolling the die and moving a corresponding number of spaces on the game board. In order to stay on a space, the player must say the word and identify the blend. If the player is correct, he stays on the space until his next turn. If the player is incorrect, he goes back two spaces on the game board. The first player to reach the finish line is the winner.

A variation of the game is played by writing the words on cards rather than on the game board. The game is played in the same manner, except that the player must choose a card and read the word from the card rather than from the game board.

49: Blend Bank

Purpose: To provide practice in identifying initial two- and three-letter blends.

Construction: Using green construction paper, cut out strips of paper that can be used as money. On each strip of paper, print a word that contains a two- or three-letter blend in the initial position. Place the strips in piles in the middle of the table. Thirty or more strips should be made.

Players: Two to four

Materials: Green construction paper, marker, scissors

Directions: The players will take turns selecting words from the pile and pronouncing them. To keep the "money," the player must say the word and identify the blend. If the player is not successful in pronouncing and identifying the blend, he must place the strip at the bottom of the pile. The player who keeps the most "money" is the winner.

50: Match Blend

Purpose: To provide practice in identifying initial two- and three-letter blends.

Construction: Use a large piece of posterboard (18″ × 13″) and attach three to eight library card pockets. Label each pocket with a two- or three-letter blend. On index cards paste pictures representing words that begin with two- or three-letter initial blends.

Example:

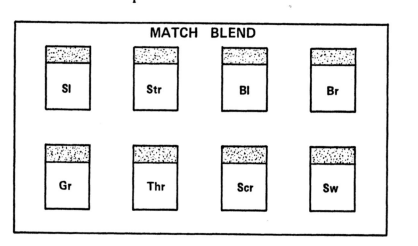

Players: One or small group

Materials: Posterboard, marker, library card pockets, index cards (3″ × 5″), pictures

Directions: Students take turns selecting picture cards and saying the blend that the picture word contains. Each picture card that is correctly named is placed in the appropriate library card pocket. The student who correctly identifies the most blends is the winner.

The game can be planned as a self-correcting activity. Print on the back of the posterboard the various blends that appear on the front. Under each blend, list the pictures that contain these blends.

51: Elephant Blend

Purpose: To provide practice in identifying final consonant blends.

Construction: Use oaktag or other stiff paper to cut out the head of an elephant with large ears. Cover the ears with clear Con-Tact paper or laminate them. Using a grease pencil, print on the ears a number of words with the final consonant blends missing. Draw a line where the blend would be written. On separate index cards (3″ × 5″) print the final consonant blends: nd, sk, mp, st, and ld.

Example:

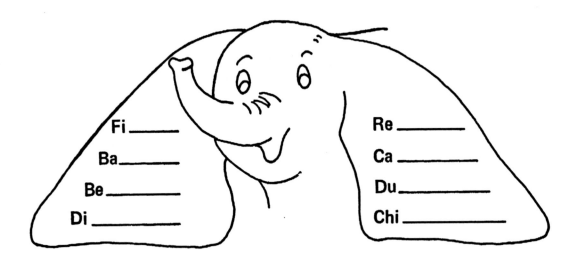

Players: Two or more

Materials: Oaktag or stiff paper, Con-Tact paper or laminating material, grease pencil, marker, index cards (3″ × 5″)

Directions: Students take turns selecting the index cards and matching them with the word parts on the elephant's ears. The student to identify the most words correctly is the winner. New words can be created by erasing the grease pencil and printing new word parts on the elephant's ears.

52: End-a-Blend

Purpose: To provide practice in identifying final consonant blends.

Construction: Make two sets of 3″ × 5″ index cards. On each card in the first set, print a word that ends with a consonant blend. For the second set of index cards, print three additional words (one word per card) that end in each final consonant blend which was used in the first set of cards.

Players: One or two

Materials: Index cards (3″ × 5″), marker

Directions: The student will select one consonant blend card from the first set of index cards. He will pronounce the word, identify the final consonant blend, and select from the second set of index cards three words that end with the same blend as in the first word.

As a variation of this activity, you can pronounce the words in the first set of cards and have the student find the three words in the second set of cards that end with the same consonant blend.

53: Story Blends

Purpose: To provide practice in identifying final consonant blends.

Construction: Select short stories that are of high interest to the children, from magazines or newspapers. Cut out these stories and paste them to stiff paper. To make the cards reusable, they should be laminated or covered with clear Con-Tact paper.

Players: One or more

Materials: Magazines, newspapers, laminating material or clear Con-Tact paper, stiff paper

Directions: Have the child select one of the stories to read, and instruct him to underline each word that ends with a consonant blend. When the child has completed the story, check the card.

To make the exercise self-correcting, the correct answers can be written on the back of the card.

54: Bees and Flowers

Purpose: To provide practice in identifying initial consonant digraphs.

Construction: Make 15 bees and 15 flowers out of felt. Attach a word that begins with an initial consonant digraph to each bee and to each flower. The words on the bees and on the flowers must correspond so that they can be matched one to one.

Example:

Players: One

Materials: Felt, marker or pen, glue

Directions: The student will match the bees and flowers that have the same initial digraphs. He will do this by placing the bee on the correct flower.

55: Alien Digraphs

Purpose: To provide practice in identifying initial consonant digraphs

Construction: Using two pieces of 8½″ × 11″ posterboard, cut each into the shape of an alien's head. Cut square eyes in one piece of the posterboard (wide enough so that strips of posterboard with letters written on them can be inserted). Attach the two head-shaped pieces together by gluing or stapling them at the ears. The strips of posterboard that have the letters on them should be approximately 1½″ × 11″ in size. On one of the strips print in a vertical line the consonant digraphs sh, ch, wh, and th. On other strips, print endings that can be matched with the consonant digraphs to make words. Each consonant digraph should have three or four strips of endings that can be matched to it. Each strip will be keyed to indicate which consonant digraph the endings will match. To key the ending strips, mark the top of the card with the consonant digraph that the endings match.

Example:

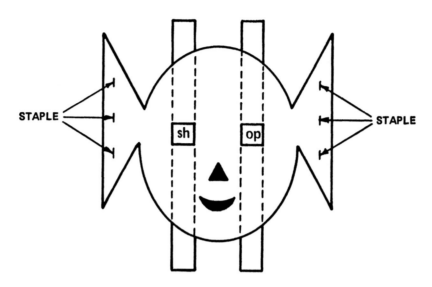

Players: One

Materials: Posterboard, marker, scissors

Directions: The student will insert two strips into the alien's head. The strip containing the consonant digraphs will be positioned behind the right eye. The other strip containing the appropriate endings will be positioned behind the left eye. The student will move the ending strip past the eye and attempt to pronounce the word that is formed.

56: Digraphs in Unison

Purpose: To provide practice in identifying initial consonant digraphs.

Construction: Write on the chalkboard a beginning consonant digraph that is to be taught. Call the students' attention to the sound it makes. List underneath the digraph four or five words that begin with that digraph.

Players: Entire class or small group

Materials: Chalkboard, chalk

Directions: Have the students pronounce in unison the words listed under the consonant digraph. When they can pronounce the words and make the appropriate sound of the digraph, ask them to say other words that begin with the same consonant digraph. All words given by the students should be written on the board and pronounced in unison by the group. Words given by the students should also be placed on index cards for future individual seatwork activities.

57: Digraph Collage

Purpose: To provide practice in identifying final consonant digraphs.

Construction: Write on the board final consonant digraphs that are to be learned. Supply the students with magazines and other materials that contain pictures. Give the students sheets of construction paper, paste, and scissors.

Players: One or entire class

Materials: Magazines, newspapers, and other sources of pictures, construction paper, paste, scissors

Directions: Instruct the students to look through the magazines and other materials to find pictures that end with the consonant digraphs listed on the board. Have the students cut out the pictures and paste them on the construction paper to make a collage. The words that are represented by the pictures will then be written at the bottom of the page. All final consonant digraphs in the words should then be underlined.

58: Match Two

Purpose: To provide practice in identifying final consonant digraphs.

Construction: Make flashcards from 3″ × 5″ index cards. Print a final consonant digraph on each of the cards. Each player will need a complete set of the digraphs being used.

Players: Two to four

Materials: Index cards (3″ × 5″), marker

Directions: Stand in front of the students and say a word that ends with a consonant digraph that is contained in the set of flashcards. After you say the word, the students must raise the index card that has the same final consonant digraph as the word you pronounced. The first student to raise the correct card must give two other words that end with the same consonant digraph. If he is sucessful, he is awarded one point. The game continues until one student has ten points.

A variation of the game is to have the student use each word in a sentence before he is awarded a point.

59: Flower Digraph

Purpose: To provide practice in identifying final consonant digraphs.

Construction: Using a large piece of posterboard, draw three or four large flowers. Attach a hook to the center of each flower. Near the bottom of each flower, attach four hooks in a horizontal line. Color the flowers bright colors. Stand the flowers in the chalk tray of the board. Using 5″ × 8″ index cards, make consonant digraph cards. Punch a hole in the middle of each card, making the holes large enough to allow the cards to hang from the hooks on the flowers. In a similar manner, make word cards from 5″ × 8″ index cards. Make eight or more word cards for each consonant digraph that is to be taught.

Example:

Players: Entire class or small group

Materials: Posterboard, hooks, crayons, marker, index cards (5″ × 8″)

Directions: Hang one of the consonant digraph cards in the middle of each of the flowers. Place the word cards in a pile in front of you. Select a card, pronounce the word, and choose a child to take the card and hang it on the bottom of the correct flower (matching the final consonant digraph) After the child hangs the card on the flower, he should say another word that ends with the same consonant digraph. If he is correct, the child returns to his chair and the activity continues. If the child is incorrect, the teacher asks another child to come to the chalk tray and correct the error. After the error is corrected, the activity continues.

60: "Y" Tree

Purpose: To provide practice in identifying "y" as a consonant.

Construction: Use a large sheet of posterboard and attach to it pieces of brown felt cut to form a tree without leaves. Cut numerous green felt leaves that can be attached to the tree, and also use a large piece of green felt to form the ground beneath the tree. To each of the leaves attach a word which begins with "y" or contains a "y." Place all the leaves with words on them in a large envelope.

Example:

Players: One or more

Materials: Posterboard, green and brown felt, pins to attach words to the leaves, envelope, marker

Directions: Instruct the child to draw a leaf from the envelope, pronounce the word, and decide whether the "y" is a vowel or a consonant. When the "y" is at the beginning of the word, it will act as a consonant and that word (leaf) will be placed on the tree. All other words which have a "y" acting as a vowel, digraph, or diphthong will be placed on the ground beneath the tree.

Sample words for "y" as a consonant are yellow, yard, yarn, yes, yeast, and yawn. The activity should be used as a reinforcement exercise after the concept of "y" has been taught. At the conclusion of the activity, all leaves on the tree will show words with "y" as a consonant.

61: Pocket "Y"

Purpose: To provide practice in identifying "y" as a consonant.

Construction: Divide a piece of posterboard in half and attach a pocket to each half. On 3" × 5" index cards, write words that have "y" serving as a consonant, vowel, digraph, or diphthong.

Example:

Y AS CONSONANT	Y AS VOWEL
yard	bay
yarn	day
yes	tray
yeast	stay
you	joy
your	happy
yours	sorry
yolk	cry
yoke	why
yell	candy
yak	fly

Players: One or more

Materials: Posterboard, marker, index cards (3" × 5"), glue

Directions: Place the cards in a pile in front of the player(s). The children take turns selecting a card, pronouncing the word, and placing it in the proper pocket. If a child mispronounces the word or places it in the incorrect pocket, it is placed on the bottom of the pile and play continues. When more than one child participate in the activity, a winner can be determined by recording the number of cards each player identifies correctly.

The activity is to be used as a means of reinforcing the "y" as a consonant concept and should be used after the concept has been taught.

62: Left-Right "C"

Purpose: To provide practice in identifying the two sounds of the letter "c."

Construction: Write on the board at the front of the room the following guide:

"C" sounds like "K" when followed by a o u Examples: cat cold cup	"C" sounds like "S" when followed by e i y Examples: cent cider cycle

On several 5″ × 8″ index cards or sheets of construction paper, print in large dark letters words beginning with "c." Vary the words so you have a good sample of "c" as "k" sounding words and "c" as "s" sounding words.

Players: Small group

Materials: Index cards (5″ × 8″) or construction paper, chalk, chalkboard, marker

Directions: Review with the group the chart on the board. Be sure to emphasize what sound the "c" will make when specified letters follow it. When the children understand the concept, hold up one of the word cards and instruct the children to raise their left hands if the "c" has a "k" sound and their right hands if the "c" has an "s" sound. Proceed through the word cards and note which children are responding correctly and which children are making errors. Children who are responding incorrectly will require further instruction and practice on the sounds of "c" activities.

63: "C" Chain

Purpose: To provide practice in identifying the two sounds of the letter "c."

Construction: Cut sheets of construction paper into strips and then cut the strips in half. On each strip, print a word that contains a "c." The "c" in the words will have either a "k" or an "s" sound.

Players: Two or more

Materials: Construction paper, marker, paste, envelopes

Directions: Divide the strips and place them in two or more envelopes. *Do not* separate them according to the sounds of "c." The children take turns choosing a strip from an envelope and pronouncing the word on the strip. After the child pronounces the word, he must identify the sound made by "c" as "k" or "s." If he correctly identifies the sound, he makes the strip into a circle and pastes the two ends together. Each successive player will add a link to the chain by intertwining the strips of paper that contain the same sounds ("k" or "s"). When the exercise is complete, two different chains will have been formed: one for the "k" sound of "c" and one for the "s" sound of "c." The activity can be made self-correcting by writing the sound the "c" makes on the backs of the strips.

64: Sound "G"

Purpose: To provide practice in identifying the two sounds of the letter "g."

Construction: Type the following guide at the top of a ditto master.

g sounds like g when followed by a o u	g sounds like j when followed by e i y (exceptions: give, girl, get, geese, gift)

Below the guide, type the following directions: In each blank, write a "g" or "j" to show the sound made by the letter "g." Type a list of words with blanks beside them below the directions.

Example:

```
gem      _____
gold     _____
garden   _____
giant    _____
gum      _____
```

Players: One child per ditto sheet

Materials: Ditto master

Directions: Instruct the children to read each word silently and decide whether the letter "g" in the word makes a "g" or "j" sound. The appropriate letter should be printed in the blank beside each word. Children who have difficulty with the exercise will need further instruction and practice with the two sounds of "g."

65: "G" Plane

Purpose: To provide practice in identifying the two sounds of the letter "g."

Construction: Cut two airplanes out of construction paper and label one "hard g" and the other "soft g." Cut sheets of construction paper into strips. Cut the strips into thirds and write words that contain a hard or soft "g" sound on the strips. Place the airplanes in the middle of a circle of children, and place all the word strips upside down in a pile on the floor.

Players: Small group

Materials: Construction paper, marker, paste

Directions: Each child in the circle will take turns selecting a word strip and pronouncing the word written on it. He will identify the sound of the "g" (hard or soft) and attach the word strip with paste to the back of the appropriately labeled airplane. Children who incorrectly identify the sound of the "g" will place that word strip at the bottom of the pile. At the completion of the exercise, each airplane will have a chain of word strips attached to it. Children who frequently miss the sound of the "g" will need further instruction and practice.

Example:

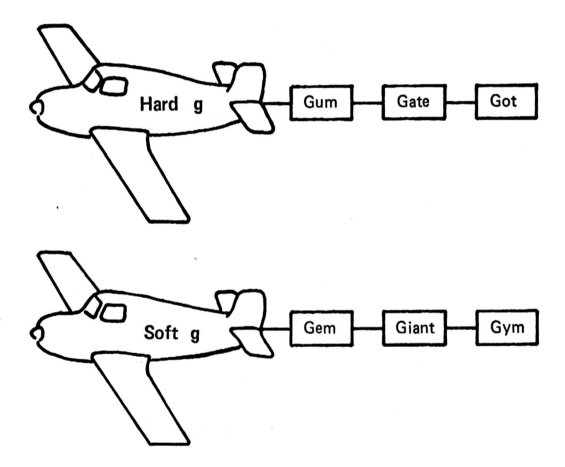

66: "S" Kites

Purpose: To provide practice in identifying the three sounds of the letter "s."

Construction: Print the following guide at the top of a large piece of posterboard:

> s in said, sale, send, sing
> z in is, his, noise, cheese
> sh in sure and sugar

Cut three kites out of construction paper and attach them in a horizontal line beneath the guide on the posterboard. Attach a hook on the bottom tip of each kite. Cut sheets of construction paper into strips, cut the strips in half, and print on each strip a word that contains one of the three sounds of the letter "s." Punch a hole in the top of each word strip. Several word strips must be made for each of the sounds of "s." Attach one or more envelopes to the bottom of the posterboard to be used for storing the word strips.

Example:

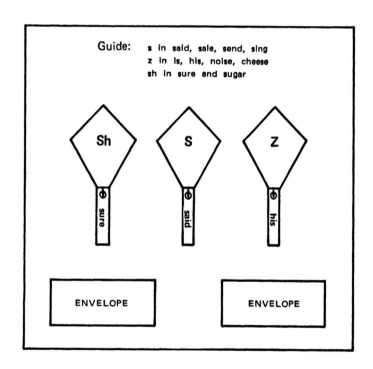

WORD LISTS

S	Sh	Z
seven		
sale	pleasure	please
ask	sugar	trees
sing	Russia	busy
siren	incision	as
say	infusion	cheese
cross		noise
sister		wise
		is

Guide: s in said, sale, send, sing
         z in is, his, noise, cheese
         sh in sure and sugar

Players: One to three

Materials: Construction paper, glue, metal or plastic hooks, scissors, marker, envelopes, posterboard.

Directions: Instruct the children to select a word strip from one of the envelopes. Each child will pronounce the word and decide what sound the "s" makes in the word (s, z, or sh). He will then hang the word strip under the appropriately labeled kite (s, z, or sh). The exercise can be made self-correcting by printing the correct sounds of "s" on an answer key.

67: "S" Track

Purpose: To provide practice in identifying the three sounds of the letter "s."

Construction: Draw an S-shaped game board on a large piece of oaktag. Divide the "S" into sections and in each section print a word containing an "s" or print directions such as "go back one space," "skip a space," etc. Each child who plays the game will have a place marker. The markers may be small cars, buttons, plastic chips, or any other appropriate objects.

Example:

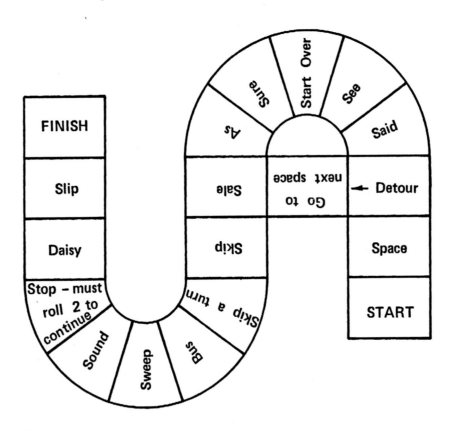

Players: Two to four

Materials: Die, large sheet of oaktag, place markers, marker

Directions: To determine the number of spaces to be moved for each turn, the players will roll the die. To stay on a space on the game board, the player must read the word printed on the space and say the correct sound of the "s" in the word. If he cannot read the word or determine the correct sound of the "s," he will go back to a space where he can read the word and correctly determine the sound of the "s." Players will also follow directions printed on various spaces of the game board such as "Take an extra turn," "Go back to Start," etc. Players take turns, and the game continues until a player crosses the finish line. The game board can be changed by printing different words in the spaces.

VOWEL RECOGNITION ACTIVITIES

The remaining activities in this section provide practice in identifying long and short vowels, the schwa sound, vowel digraphs, and vowel diphthongs, and in recognizing vowel rules and vowel rule exceptions.

68: Turkey Feather Vowels

Purpose: To provide practice in identifying long and short vowels.

Construction: Make ten turkeys out of construction paper. Cut strips of construction paper into feathers that can be used for the tail, but do not attach them to the bodies of the turkeys. Label each of the turkeys with a vowel (a,e,i,o,u)—five with long vowels and five with short vowels. On each tail feather, print a word with a long vowel sound or a word with a short vowel sound. Make several tail feathers for each vowel sound. In words that contain two or more vowels, underline the vowel to be identified as long or short. Place the turkeys and the tail feathers on a large table.

Players: Two or more

Materials: Construction paper, scissors, marker

Directions: Players take turns selecting a tail feather from the pile on the table, pronouncing the word printed on it, and deciding whether the word has a long or short vowel sound. If the word has been correctly pronounced and the vowel sound correctly identified, the tail feather will be placed in the tail of the turkey which is labeled with the appropriate long or short vowel. For example, the tail feather with the word "cane" printed on it will be placed on the turkey labeled "long a." If a word is mispronounced or if the vowel sound is identified incorrectly, that tail feather is placed at the bottom of the pile.

69: Vowel Boats

Purpose: To provide practice in identifying long and short vowels.

Construction: Using construction paper, cut out ten boats and glue each boat to the front of a shoe box. Label five of the boats with the long vowels and five of the boats with the short vowels. On 3″ × 5″ index cards, print words that have long vowels and words that have short vowels. If the word has more than one vowel, underline the vowel to be identified as long or short.

Players: Two to four

Materials: Ten shoe boxes, construction paper, scissors, glue, marker, index cards (3″ × 5″)

Directions: Place the index cards in a pile in the middle of a large table. Place the shoe boxes in a line on the table. The players will take turns selecting a card, reading the word, identifying the vowel sound as long or short, and placing the card in the appropriate "vowel boat." If a word is read incorrectly or if a vowel is identified incorrectly, the card will be placed on the bottom of the pile. At the conclusion of the activity, the word cards in each "vowel boat" may be read by the players as further reinforcement of the long and short vowel sounds.

70: Vowel Road

Purpose: To provide practice in identifying long and short vowels.

Construction: On a large sheet of posterboard draw a game board and divide it into several sections. In each section print a long or short vowel word or print directions such as "Pothole: Skip a turn," "Detour: Go back one space," "Accident: Skip two turns," "Passing Zone: Advance two spaces," etc. On 3″ × 5″ index cards, print long and short vowel words. In words that contain two or more vowels, underline the vowel to be identified as long or short. For each of the long and short vowels make ten or more word cards.

Example:

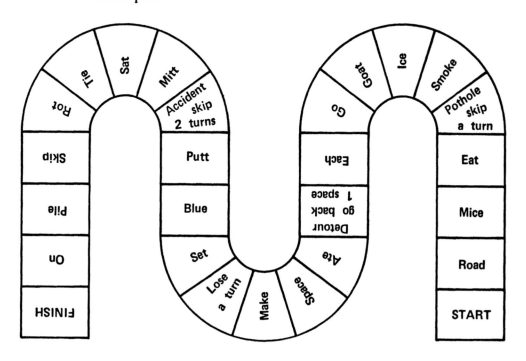

Players: Two to four

Materials: Posterboard, place markers, marker, index cards (3″ × 5″), die

Directions: Each player selects a card, pronounces the word printed on it, and identifies the sound of the vowel as long or short. If he successfully accomplishes this, he will be permitted to roll the die and advance his marker the indicated number of spaces on the game board. To stay on the space, the player must read the word, give the correct sound of the vowel, and say another word that has the same vowel sound. If the player lands on a space that has a direction (such as "Pothole: Skip a turn") instead of a word, he will follow the direction. The first player to reach the finish line on the game board is the winner.

71: Squirrels and Acorns Match Game

Purpose: To provide practice in identifying long and short vowels.

Construction: Using construction paper, cut out squirrels and acorns, making them about the size of playing cards. Print a word on each squirrel and each acorn. Have several words for each of the long and short vowels. In words that contain two or more vowels, underline the vowel that is to be identified as long or short. The vowel sounds on the squirrels and acorns must match one-to-one.

Players: Two or more

Materials: Construction paper, scissors, marker

Directions: Place the squirrels and acorns in two separate piles in the middle of a table. Instruct the players to select a squirrel and an acorn. If the vowel sounds match, place the acorn on top of the squirrel. For example, the squirrel with "kite" would match the acorn with "right." Each player places his matches on the table in front of him. If the squirrel and acorn do not match, the player will keep them in his hand for future use. The players take turns until all the squirrels and acorns have been matched. The player with the most matches is the winner.

72: Vowel Bones

Purpose: To provide practice in identifying long and short vowels.

Construction: Take construction paper and cut out a dog and ten dog dishes. Paste the dog to the center of a large sheet of posterboard. Paste the dog dishes in vertical lines, five on either side of the dog. When pasting the dog dishes, leave the tops open so that paper bones can be placed in the dishes. Print one of the vowels above each of the dog dishes. All long vowels should be printed above the dishes on the left and all short vowels above the dishes on the right. Make numerous bones out of white construction paper and print words with long or short vowels on each of the bones. In words which contain more than one vowel, underline the vowel to be identified as long or short.

Example:

FEED THE DOG

Players: Two to four

Materials: Posterboard, construction paper, scissors, paste, marker

Directions: Players take turns selecting a bone, pronouncing the word printed on it, and identifying the vowel as being long or short. If the word is pronounced correctly and the vowel correctly identified, the bone is placed in the dog dish that is labeled with the appropriate long or short vowel. If a word is mispronounced or a vowel is incorrectly identified, the bone is placed at the bottom of the pile. When the activity has been completed, the players may read the words on the bones in each dog dish to reinforce each long and short vowel sound

73: Baseball Vowels

Purpose: To provide practice in identifying long and short vowels.

Construction: Using construction paper, cut out ten baseball hats and print one long or short vowel on each. Attach the hats to the bulletin board or to a wall in the room. In hanging the hats, place the long vowel above the short vowel (long e above short e, long a above short a, etc.). Leave space below each hat for 15 word cards in the shape of baseballs. Cut baseballs out of construction paper and print a word that contains a long or short vowel on each. In words that contain more than one vowel, underline the one to be identified as long or short.

Players: Two to four

Materials: Construction paper, scissors, marker, paper clips

Directions: Players will take turns selecting baseballs from a pile and pronouncing the word printed on each. The player must identify the vowel as being long or short and hang it with a paper clip under the appropriately labeled baseball hat. If a word is mispronounced, or if a vowel is incorrectly identified, the word card (baseball) is placed at the bottom of the pile.

74: Schwa Pocket

Purpose: To provide practice in identifying the schwa sound.

Construction: To make a large posterboard pocket, staple together two half-circles 20 inches in diameter. Using 5″ × 8″ index cards, print a word on the front of each card and the definition of the word on the back of the card. When printing the word on the front of the card, omit a vowel (long, short, or schwa). Make numerous cards for each vowel sound (long, short, schwa). Place all the cards in a pile on a table.

Example:

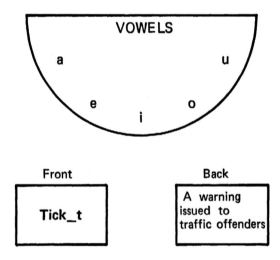

Players: Two or more

Materials: Posterboard, marker, index cards (5″ × 8″), scissors, stapler

Directions: Read to each player the definition of a word that is on the back of one of the index cards. He will try to guess the word from the definition. When he says the correct word, allow him to look at the word on the front of the card and supply the missing vowel. After identifying the missing vowel, the student must tell if the vowel's sound is long, short, or schwa. If he is correct, the card is placed in the posterboard pocket. If he is incorrect, the card is placed at the bottom of the card file.

The students will enjoy playing the game if the words are ones that they have studied in their reading lessons.

75: Schwa Search

Purpose: To provide practice in identifying the schwa sound.

Construction: On a ditto master, construct sentences that have words that contain the schwa sound. Write numerous sentences on the ditto master.

Players: One child per ditto sheet

Materials: Ditto master

Directions: The children read the sentences and circle all schwa sounds contained in the words. All words containing vowels that are incorrectly circled will be placed on flash cards and used for future practice.

76: Digraph Hopscotch

Purpose: To provide practice in identifying vowel digraphs.

Construction: With masking tape, make a hopscotch pattern on the floor. Inside each square, tape a 5″ × 8″ index card with a vowel digraph printed on it. Use beanbags to toss in the hopscotch squares.

Players: Two to four

Materials: Masking tape, marker, index cards (5″ × 8″), beanbags

Directions: The player throws the beanbag on the first square and proceeds to hop on the other squares as in hopscotch. Before he can pick up his beanbag on the first square, he must say two words that contain the vowel digraph written in that square. He repeats this procedure until he misses a word or wins the game. All rules for regular hopscotch apply to this game. The winner is the player who completes the game first.

77: Digraph Houses

Purpose: To provide practice in identifying vowel digraphs.

Construction: Make houses out of construction paper and print one vowel digraph on each of them. Make a house for each vowel digraph that is to be used. Paste a pocket on the front of each house so that 3″ × 5″ index cards can be placed in it. Make a barn out of construction paper, and print "Barn" on it. On 3″ × 5″ index cards print numerous words that contain the vowel digraphs which are to be practiced.

Players: Two or more

Materials: Construction paper, scissors, paste, marker, index cards (3″ × 5″)

Directions: Give each of the digraph houses to a student to hold. Place the barn on the chalk tray. The children holding the houses will act as doorkeepers for the houses. Players take turns choosing a card from the pile and saying to the doorkeeper of the house that matches the digraph contained on the word card, "May I visit your house?" The doorkeeper answers, "Yes, if your card matches my house. What sound does it make?" The child responds by saying the word and identifying the vowel digraph in his word. All correct words are placed in the pocket of the correct house. If the child has answered incorrectly, his word card is placed in the "Barn." At the end of the exercise all words which are found in the barn are retaught or reviewed with the students.

78: Digraph Match

Purpose: To provide practice in identifying vowel digraphs

Construction: Across the top of a large piece of posterboard, paste pictures of objects that contain vowel digraphs in their spelling (goat, seat, etc.). The pictures may be cut from magazines or drawn by you. Attach hooks in a vertical line under each picture. Leave space below each of the hooks for a word card to hang. Cut construction paper squares or circles that can be used as word cards. Punch a hole in the top of each card, and print on the card a word that contains one of the vowel digraphs pictured at the top of the posterboard.

Example:

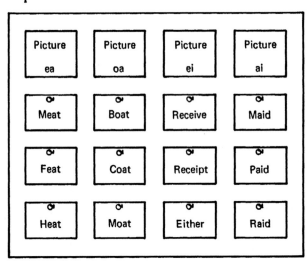

Players: Two

Materials: Posterboard, construction paper, paste, scissors, hooks, marker

Directions: Place the word cards in a pile and have the players take turns selecting a card. After they select a word card, they must pronounce the word and identify the vowel digraph in the word. If they correctly pronounce the word and identify the vowel digraph, they will hang the card on a hook under the correct picture. If a word is mispronounced or the vowel digraph identified incorrectly, that word card is placed at the bottom of the pile.

79: Diphthong Match

Purpose: To provide practice in identifying vowel diphthongs.

Construction: On a ditto master, list words containing vowel diphthongs in a column on the left side of the page. In a column on the right side of the page, list in random order words that contain the same vowel diphthongs as those words on the left.

Players: One child per ditto sheet

Materials: Ditto master

Directions: The student will match the words in the right column with those in the left column that have the same diphthongs. The student will identify the matching words by drawing a line between them.

The activity is to be used as a means of reinforcing the student's understanding of vowel diphthongs and should be used after the diphthongs have been taught.

80: Diphthong Owls

Purpose: To provide practice in identifying vowel diphthongs.

Construction: On each of three or more sheets of posterboard, draw a large tree without leaves. On the trunk of each tree print a different vowel diphthong (oi, ow, oy, ou, etc.). Attach the posterboards to a large bulletin board. Using different colored construction paper, cut out owls that are large enough to be placed on the branches of the trees. On each owl, print a word that contains one of the diphthongs printed on the tree trunks.

Players: Two to four

Materials: Posterboard, construction paper, scissors, marker, thumbtacks

Directions: Place the owls in a pile and have the players take turns selecting an owl. After a player selects an owl, he must pronounce the word and identify the vowel diphthong contained in the word. If he correctly pronounces the word and identifies the diphthong, he will thumbtack the owl to a branch of the tree that has the same vowel diphthong printed on its trunk. If a word is mispronounced or if a diphthong is incorrectly identified, the owl is placed at the bottom of the pile. At the conclusion of the activity, the players may read the words attached to each tree to reinforce the sound of each vowel diphthong.

81: Picture Diphthongs

Purpose: To provide practice in identifying vowel diphthongs.

Construction: On a ditto master, type or print words that contain vowel diphthongs. Cut pictures from magazines or draw pictures of objects that contain the same diphthongs as the words listed on the ditto. Paste the pictures on construction paper.

Players: Large group

Materials: Ditto master, construction paper, scissors, paste

Directions: Distribute a copy of the ditto sheet to all players. Stand in front of the group and show them the pictures. Direct them to look at the picture, pronounce silently the word it represents, and then place a number beside one word on the ditto sheet that has the same diphthong as the word pictured. As you show the pictures, the students will sequentially number their words to correspond to the order of presentation of the pictures (number one to match the first picture, number two for the second picture, etc.). Their ditto sheet and your pictures will contain several examples of the same diphthongs. Continue the activity until all the pictures have been shown.

By collecting the sheets and checking the numbers written beside each word, you can determine which children need more practice with diphthongs.

82: Hang Vowel

Purpose: To provide practice in recognizing CVC, CVCe, CVVC, and CV vowel rules when applied.

Construction: Across the top of a sheet of posterboard draw and label three pictures—one each of "Mr. Long," "Mr. Short," and "Mr. Silent." Draw the pictures like cartoon characters. Divide the posterboard vertically into three equal parts under each of the characters at the top. Under "Mr. Long," paste eleven picture hooks. Under "Mr. Short," paste five picture hooks, and under "Mr. Silent," paste four picture hooks. On circles cut from construction paper, write five words for the CVC rule and underline the vowels; write five words for the CVCe rule and underline the vowel in three words and the *e* in two words. Write five words for the CVVC rule and underline the first vowel in three words and the second vowel in two words. Write five words for the CV rule and underline the vowel. Punch holes in the tops of the circles.

Players: Two

Materials: Posterboard, construction paper, picture hooks, marker

Directions: The players will take turns selecting a circle from the pile. They will pronounce the word aloud and identify the underlined vowel as long, short, or silent. If the player correctly identifies the vowel sound, he will hang the circle on the picture hook under the correct column (long, short, or silent). If the word is mispronounced or the vowel incorrectly identified, the word circle will be placed at the bottom of the pile.

83: Vowel Card Challenge

Purpose: To provide practice in recognizing CVC, CVCe, CVVC, and CV vowel rules when applied.

Construction: Write 15 words for each of the CVC, CVCe, CVVC, and CV rules on 3″ × 5″ index cards. Underline one of the vowels in each of the words.

Players: Two to four

Materials: Index cards (3″ × 5″), marker, a die

Directions: The players roll the die to determine who goes first, second, third, and fourth. They take turns selecting a card and pronouncing the word written on it. After a player pronounces the word correctly and correctly identifies the underlined vowel as long, short, or silent, he will say two other words that have the same vowel sound. If the words given are correct, the player may keep the word card. If he is incorrect, he will place the card at the bottom of the pile. The winner of the game is the player with the most cards.

84: Team Vowels

Purpose: To provide practice in recognizing CVC, CVCe, CVVC, and CV vowel rules when applied.

Construction: On several 3″ × 5″ index cards write words that follow the CVC, CVCe, CVVC, and CV vowel rules. Underline one vowel in each word. Place the word cards in a pile on a table.

Players: Two teams of four players each

Materials: Index cards (3″ × 5″), marker

Directions: Players on opposite teams will take turns selecting a word card from the pile. They will pronounce the word aloud and identify the underlined vowel as being long, short, or silent. If the player's answer is correct, his team will be awarded one point. If the player's answer is incorrect, the card is placed at the bottom of the pile and no points are awarded. The winning team is the one with the most points at the conclusion of the game.

85: Vowel Rule Match

Purpose: To provide practice in recognizing CVC, CVCe, CVVC, and CV vowel rules when applied.

Construction: On each of four 5″ × 8″ index cards, write one of the vowel rules— CVC, CVCe, CVVC, and CV. Attach each of the cards to the front of a paper milk carton with the top removed. Using oaktag cut out four imaginary cartoon-type characters. Attach them to the fronts of the milk cartons for color and decoration. On several 3″ × 5″ index cards print words that follow the CVC, CVCe, CVVC, or CV vowel rules. Place the cartons in a row on a table, and place the word cards in a pile in front of the cartons.

Players: One

Materials: Index cards (5″ × 8″ and 3″ × 5″), four paper milk cartons, oaktag, scissors, glue, marker, stapler

Directions: The player selects a word card from the pile, pronounces the word aloud, and matches the word with the rule on one of the milk cartons. He will then deposit the word card in the appropriately labeled carton. The exercise can be made self-checking by writing on a scoring sheet the rules and the words that follow each rule.

You should review the rules and do several examples with the student before he begins the exercise.

86: Hang the Word

Purpose: To provide practice in recognizing CVC, CVCe, CVVC, and CV vowel rules when applied.

Construction: Divide a piece of posterboard into four sections. At the top of each section write one of the vowel rules—CVC, CVCe, CVVC, and CV. Attach six picture hooks in a vertical line below each rule. Print several words that follow each of the vowel rules on 3″ × 5″ index cards. Punch holes in the top of the index cards.

Players: One or two

Materials: Posterboard, picture books, index cards (3″ × 5″), marker

Directions: The players take turns selecting cards and pronouncing the word on the card. After pronouncing the word, the player identifies the vowel rule that the word matches, and hangs the card on a hook in the appropriate column. Before starting the exercise, you should review the vowel rules with the players.

87: Vowel Rule Match

Purpose: To provide practice in identifying words that contain an "o" followed by "ld" or "lt," an "a" followed by "l," "ll," "w," or "u" and an "i" followed by "nd," "gh," or "ld."

Construction: On each of three large word cards (8½″ × 11″) print one of the vowel rule exceptions that is to be practiced. On 5″ × 8″ index cards print a word that matches one of the rules. Make several cards for each of the rules.

Players: Two or small group

Materials: Word cards (8½″ × 11″), index cards (5″ × 8″), marker

Directions: Place the three rule cards in a row on the chalk tray. Place all of the word cards in a pile on a table. Each player will select a card from the pile and pronounce the word printed on it. If he pronounces the word correctly, he will then identify the rule card that the word matches. He will place the word card on the chalk tray behind the correct rule card. If he mispronounces the word, he will place the word card at the bottom of the pile. The players will receive one point for each word *missed*. The winner is the player with the least points. The game may also be played by dividing a small group of children into two teams.

You should review the rules with the players before beginning the activity.

88: Vowel Baseball

Purpose: To provide practice in identifying words that contain an "o" followed by "ld" or "lt," an "a" followed by "l," "ll," "w," or "u" and an "i" followed by "nd," "gh," or "ld."

Construction: Draw a baseball diamond on the chalkboard. Using two different colors of construction paper, cut out eight figures of baseball players (four men for each color) to be used as base runners on the baseball diamond. Attach double-face adhesive mounting tape to the back of each figure. Make word cards using 3″ × 5″ index cards.

On numerous cards, print words that match the rules to be practiced. You should make several cards for each of the vowel rule exceptions. Place the cards in a pile on a table.

Players: Two teams of players

Materials: Chalkboard, chalk, construction paper, double-face adhesive mounting tape, index cards 3″ × 5″, marker

Directions: Two teams of players are selected. Each team is given one set of the baseball player figures that will be used as base runners in the game. The game is played like baseball, except that the only hit is a single. Players on the team at bat will take turns selecting cards from the pile. Each batter will pronounce the word, identify the vowel exception in the word, and give one other word that contains the same vowel exception. If the player does this successfully, he scores a hit and his base runner is placed on first base. If he is unsuccessful, an out is scored. As successive players come to bat, runs will be scored and outs will be recorded. The process continues until three outs are made. The next team will then take its turn at bat. You may make the game last as many innings as you wish. The winning team is the team that scores the most runs in the game.

89: Quick Thinking

Purpose: To provide practice in identifying words that contain an "o" followed by "ld" or "lt," an "a" followed by "l," "ll," "w," or "u" and an "i" followed by "nd," "gh," or ld."

Construction: On each 3″ × 5″ index card, print a word that contains an "o" followed by "ld" or "lt," an "a" followed by "l," "ll," "w," or "u" or an "i" followed by "nd," "gh," or "ld." Make numerous word cards for each vowel rule exception.

Players: Four or more

Materials: Index cards (3″ × 5″), marker

Directions: Place the cards face down in the middle of a table. Players take turns selecting cards from the pile, identifying the vowel exception, and giving another word that contains the same vowel exception. The player must accomplish this task before five seconds have elapsed. If he successfully does this, he may keep the card; if he is not successful, he must place the card at the bottom of the pile. The winner is the player who accumulates the most cards.

90: "R" Vowel Match

Purpose: To provide practice in identifying words that contain a vowel followed by an "r."

Construction: Label the outside of each of four plastic egg cartons with one of the different letter combinations for r-controlled vowels (ir, er, ar, and or). Cut out numerous construction paper circles that can fit inside the egg carton. On each circle, print a word that has one of the r-controlled vowels contained in it.

Players: One or two

Materials: Four plastic egg cartons, construction paper, scissors, marker

Directions: Place the construction paper circles in a pile on the table. The player will select a circle, pronounce the word printed on it, and place it in the correct egg carton according to the r-controlled vowel contained in the word. The exercise should be used as a review activity.

91: Tic Tac R

Purpose: To provide practice in identifying words which contain a vowel followed by an "r."

Construction: On a sheet of paper draw a tic tac toe game board. Using construction paper, cut out 18 squares of paper that can be used as markers on the game board. Write X's on nine of the markers and O's on the remaining nine. Use several 3″ × 5″ index cards to make word cards. On each card, print a word that contains one of the following vowels followed by an "r": o, e, i, a. Place the cards in a pile on a table.

Players: Two

Materials: Large sheet of paper, construction paper, scissors, marker, index cards (3″ × 5″)

Directions: The players take turns selecting cards from the card pile. After selecting a card, the player must pronounce the word and identify the r-controlled vowel contained in the word. If he is successful in doing this, he must then say two other words that contain the same r-controlled vowel. If he is also successful with this task, he may place one of his markers (X or O) on a tic tac toe space of his choice. The exercise continues until one player wins the tic tac toe game. A game that is not won by either player is called a draw and a new game is started.

92: "Y" Rule Match

Purpose: To provide practice in identifying "y" as a vowel.

Construction: Using four large-group-size flash cards (8½″ × 11″), print one of the following rules on each of the four cards:

1. "y" acts as a vowel when it is part of the vowel digraph "ay" (may, hay, etc.)
2. "y" acts as a vowel when it is part of the vowel diphthong "oy" (destroy, boy, etc.)
3. "y" acts as a vowel when it concludes a word of two or more syllables (hobby, lucky, etc.)
4. "y" acts as a vowel when it comes at the end of a word that contains no other vowels (my, shy, etc.)

On 5″ × 8″ index cards, print words that follow the four "y" rules. Make several cards for each rule.

Players: Two or small group

Materials: Posterboard (8½″ × 11″), index cards (5″ × 8″), marker

Directions: Place the four rule cards in a row on the chalk tray. Place all of the word cards in a pile on a table. Each player will take turns selecting a card from the pile and pronouncing the word written on it. If he correctly pronounces the word, he will identify the "y" rule that the word matches, and place the word on the chalk tray behind the correct rule card. If he is incorrect, he will place the word card at the bottom of the pile. The players will receive one point for every word *missed*. The winner is the player with the least points.

Before starting the activity, review with the players the four "y" rules and some sample words for each rule.

93: "Y" Rule Flower

Purpose: To provide practice in identifying "y" as a vowel.

Construction: Using construction paper, cut out four large circles. The circles will be used as centers for large flowers. On each circle print one of the following rules:

1. "y" acts as a vowel when it is part of the vowel digraph "ay" (may, hay, etc.)
2. "y" acts as a vowel when it is part of the vowel diphthong "oy" (destroy, boy, etc.)
3. "y" acts as a vowel when it concludes a word of two or more syllables (hobby, lucky, etc.)
4. "y" acts as a vowel when it comes at the end of a word that contains no other vowels (my, shy, etc.)

Cut flower petals from strips of construction paper, and print on each a word that follows one of the above-listed rules. Make several flower petals for each "y" rule.

Players: One to four

Materials: Construction paper, scissors, paste or brass fasteners, marker

Directions: Place the flower centers in a row on a large table. Place the petals beside the flower centers. Each player will select a petal and pronounce the word printed on it. If he is correct, he will identify the flower center rule that the petal matches. He will then attach the petal to the appropriate flower center. If he is incorrect, he will return the petal to the pile on the table, placing it on the bottom of the pile. The players will receive one point for each petal that they match to the correct rule. The winner is the player who accumulates the most points.

You should review the rules for "y" as a vowel before the players begin the activity.

Section 3

ACTIVITIES TO IMPROVE STRUCTURAL ANALYSIS AND SYLLABICATION

STRUCTURAL ANALYSIS ACTIVITIES

The following activities teach the pupil to recognize small words in compound words and to identify inflectional endings, root words, contractions, possessives, and plurals.

94: Compound Match

Purpose: To provide practice in recognizing small words in compound words.

Construction: Print compound words on strips of construction paper. Leave space between the two small words within the compound word so that the paper strip can be cut in half. When you cut the strip of paper, use a zigzag motion. The zigzag design will serve as a guide for putting the two halves back together. Do not use more than ten compound words at a time. Mix the halves and place them in a pile on a table.

Players: One

Materials: Construction paper, scissors, marker

Directions: The player will select two pieces from the pile and fit the halves together to form a compound word. After the word is formed, the student will pronounce the word aloud. The player can check his answer by seeing whether or not the puzzle pieces fit together.

95: Compound Frog Fun

Purpose: To provide practice in recognizing small words in compound words.

Construction: Make several lily pads out of green construction paper. Print the last half of a compound word on each lily pad and make a slit in each lily pad above the word. Make several frogs out of brown construction paper, and print the first half of a compound word on each frog to correspond with the lily pads. When cutting out each frog, leave a piece of construction paper sticking out on the bottom (like a tab) so that it can be placed into the slit cut in the lily pad. Place the frogs and the lily pads in separate piles on a table.

Players: One or two

Materials: Construction paper (green and brown), scissors, marker

Directions: The player will match the frogs with the correct lily pads to form compound words. You can make the exercise self-correcting by preparing an answer sheet.

96: Compound Pictures

Purpose: To provide practice in recognizing small words in compound words.

Construction: Cut pictures of compound words out of magazines (streetcar, snowman, butterfly, evergreen, etc.). Attach the pictures to oaktag paper. Take 3″ × 5″ index cards and print the first half of the compound word on one card and the second half of the word on another card. Place the picture cards and the two sets of index cards in three piles on a table.

Players: Two

Materials: Pictures cut from magazines, oaktag, index cards (3″ × 5″), scissors, marker

Directions: Players take turns selecting a picture and pronouncing the compound word that it represents. After they have correctly identified the picture, they will find the two 3″ × 5″ index cards that contain the first and second halves of the compound word. If a player cannot find the correct cards, he replaces the picture card in the appropriate pile. The exercise can be made self-correcting by printing the compound word on the back of the picture.

97: Inflectional Triangle

Purpose: To provide practice in identifying words with inflectional endings.

Construction: Draw a large triangle game board on a piece of posterboard. Divide the game board into sections and print an inflectional ending in each section (s, ing, er, ed, etc.). Using a small piece of posterboard, make a spinner and print the numbers 1 to 4 on it. Players can use buttons or other small objects for place markers.

Example:

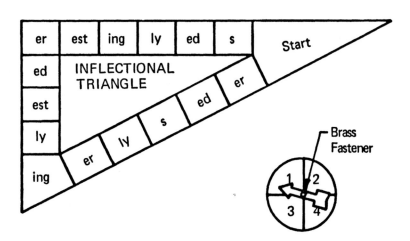

Players: Two or three

Materials: Posterboard, marker, buttons or other small objects for place markers, brass fastener

Directions: The players place their markers on the section of the game board marked "Start." Players take turns spinning the spinner and moving the correct number of sections on the game board. To stay on a section, the player must say two words that end with the inflectional ending printed in that section. If the player cannot give two correct words, he returns to his previous place on the board. The first player to go around the game board twice is the winner.

98: Inflectional Worm

Purpose: To provide practice in identifying words with inflectional endings.

Construction: Using oaktag, cut out heads for six worms and print one of the following inflectional endings on each head: er, est, ly, s, ed, and ing. Attach the heads to a large bulletin board and leave enough space behind each head for several circles (body parts) to be added. Using brightly colored construction paper, cut numerous large circles and print a noun, verb, or adjective on each circle. The words on the circles must match one of the inflectional endings on the worm heads.

Players: Entire class

Materials: Oaktag, construction paper, scissors, marker or crayons, thumbtacks

Directions: The players take turns selecting a circle that can be added behind the appropriate worm head. The player pronounces the word on the circle, decides which inflectional ending may be correctly added to it, and then pronounces the word created when the ending is added to the word on the circle. The player then tacks the circle to the bulletin board behind the appropriate worm head. The object of the activity is to make long worms for each ending.

A variation of the activity is to assign the worm heads to the children in small groups or by rows. The children in each group or row will attempt to find words for their worm head. The winner is the group or row that makes the longest worm.

99: Inflectional Pockets

Purpose: To provide practice in identifying words with inflectional endings.

Construction: Using six 3″ × 5″ index cards, print one of the following inflectional endings on each card: ed, er, ly, ing, est, and s. Place one inflectional ending card at the top of each column of a pocket chart. Using additional 3″ × 5″ index cards, print a word that can be matched to one of the inflectional endings on each card. Place the word cards in a pile on a table by the chart.

Example:

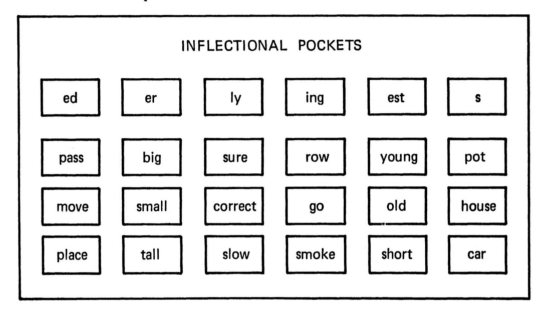

Players: Two to four

Materials: Pocket chart, index cards (3″ × 5″), marker

Directions: The players take turns choosing a word and placing it in the pocket under the correct inflectional ending. The player must also pronounce the word that is formed by adding the ending. If the word is placed in an incorrect pocket or is mispronounced, the word card is placed at the bottom of the pile.

100: Root Word Roundup

Purpose: To provide practice in recognizing the root word from the suffix, prefix, or both affixes.

Construction: Make several horses out of construction paper. On the horses, print root words that have prefixes, suffixes, or both affixes added (one word on each horse). Place the horses in a pile on a table.

Players: Two to four

Materials: Construction paper, scissors, marker

Directions: The players take turns selecting a horse from the pile, pronouncing the word printed on it, and identifying the root word. If the player is correct, he will keep the horse. If his answer is incorrect, he will place the horse at the bottom of the pile. The winner of the exercise is the player who "rounds up" the most horses.

101: Root Word Butterfly

Purpose: To provide practice in recognizing the root word from the suffix, prefix, or both affixes.

Construction: Cut several large butterflies out of oaktag or other heavy paper. Using words that have both prefixes and suffixes, print a word on each butterfly as follows: prefix on the left wing, root word on the body, and suffix on the right wing. Cut each butterfly into three pieces: two wings and the body. Place the three sections in three different containers: prefixes, root words, suffixes. The containers may be made from shoe boxes, plastic bowls, milk cartons, etc. and should be clearly labeled "Prefixes," "Root Words," and "Suffixes."

Players: Individual or small group

Materials: Oaktag, scissors, marker, three containers (shoe boxes, plastic bowls, milk cartons, etc.)

Directions: The player selects a root word from the "Root Word" container and attempts to match it with the appropriate prefix/suffix wings. If he finds the correct wings, a word will be formed and he will keep the butterfly. If he cannot find the correct wings to match the body, he will keep the body and return the wings to their containers.

You can check to see what words are not understood by checking which bodies and wings are left or incorrectly matched.

102: Root Word Road

Purpose: To provide practice in recognizing the root word from the suffix, prefix, or both affixes.

Construction: Draw an S-shaped road on a piece of posterboard or other stiff paper. At the end of the road, draw a castle. Divide the road into sections, and in each section print a root word with a prefix and/or suffix added to it.

Example:

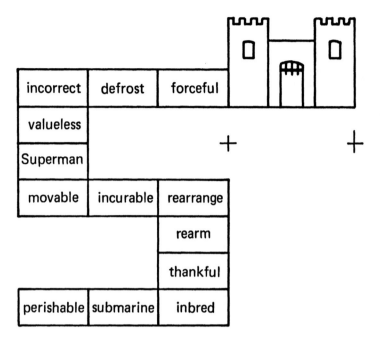

incorrect	defrost	forceful
valueless		
Superman		
movable	incurable	rearrange
		rearm
		thankful
perishable	submarine	inbred

Players: Two to four

Materials: Posterboard or other stiff paper, marker, place markers, die

Directions: The players will take turns rolling a die and moving their markers the indicated number of spaces on the road. To stay on the space, the player must say the word and identify the root word. If his answer is incorrect, he must move back one space. The first player to reach the castle is the winner.

103: Contraction Action

Purpose: To provide practice in identifying contractions.

Construction: Write contractions and their corresponding word forms on separate 3″ × 5″ index cards. The contractions and their word forms may be repeated on more than one pair of cards.

Players: Two to four

Materials: Index cards (3″ × 5″), marker

Directions: Every player is dealt an equal number of cards. The players check their cards to identify any matches that may have been dealt to them.

Cards that match are placed on the table in front of each player. Players take turns choosing a card from the player to the right. Each player attempts to match either a contraction or word form on the cards in his hand to the card that he selects from the player on his right. For example, if the player chooses a card with *is not*, he has a match if he has the card with *isn't* in his hand. If the player has a match, he places the two cards on the table in front of him and he takes another turn. If the player does not make a match, he adds the card he selected to the cards in his hand. The player who is the first to match all his cards is the winner.

104: Tic Tac Concentration

Purpose: To provide practice in identifying contractions.

Construction: Draw a tic tac toe board on a piece of oaktag or other stiff paper. Using 3″ × 5″ index cards, make two cards for each contraction. Mark an X on one contraction card and an O on the other. Place all the X contraction cards in one envelope and all the O contraction cards in another. Print the word forms that correspond to the contractions on separate index cards. The word form cards are placed in each tic tac toe square of the game board.

Players: Two

Materials: Oaktag or other stiff paper, index cards (3″ × 5″), marker, two envelopes

Directions: Each player is given an envelope with the contraction cards. One player will have all the X cards and the other will have all the O cards. The players take turns selecting a contraction card, reading the contraction, and matching it with the corresponding word form on the game board. If the player can correctly read the contraction and match it to the corresponding word form on the game board, he places his X or O contraction card over the word form on the game board. The first player to get three X's or O's in a row (across, down, or diagonally) is the winner.

105: Spell a Contraction

Purpose: To provide practice in identifying contractions.

Construction: Print the corresponding word form for a contraction on each of thirty 5″ × 8″ index cards. For example, you will print is not, can not, you have, she will, etc.

Players: Two or three

Materials: Index cards (5″ × 8″), marker

Directions: The players take turns selecting a card, reading the words printed on it, identifying the contraction form of the words, and correctly spelling the contraction. If the player gives the correct answer, he places the card in front of him and receives one point. If the player gives an incorrect answer, he places the card on the bottom of the pile. The player with the most points at the end of the exercise is the winner.

106: Possessive Match

Purpose: To provide practice in using possessives in context.

Construction: On a ditto master, type thirty sentences that show possession. Under each of these sentences type another sentence that contains a possessive noun. For example, the first sentence would read "This dog belongs to Steve." The second sentence would read "This is (Steves, Steve's) dog."

Players: Entire class

Materials: Ditto master

Directions: The students read each sentence silently and circle the correct possessive form. By preparing an answer key, the activity can be made self-correcting.

107: Pick a Possessive

Purpose: To provide practice in recognizing possessive pronouns.

Construction: On strips of construction paper, print sentences that contain possessive pronouns. For example, you would print "We are near his house."

Players: One

Materials: Construction paper, marker, scissors, small round markers (plastic chips, buttons, pennies, etc.)

Directions: The student reads the sentence and places a plastic chip over the possessive pronoun contained in the sentence. If desired, the student can circle the possessive pronoun rather than using a small object to cover it.

108: Possessive Clip

Purpose: To provide practice in recognizing possessives in context.

Construction: Write a sentence on each of several strips of oaktag. The sentences should contain a choice of two answers: one a possessive and the other a plural. For example, "The black and white kitten is Johns/John's."

Players: One

Materials: Oaktag strips, marker, paper clips

Directions: The student reads the sentence on each strip and identifies the correct answer by placing a paper clip over it (or by circling it). The exercise can be made self-correcting by writing the correct answer on the back of each strip.

109: Plural Football

Purpose: To provide practice in forming "s," "es," "ies," and "ves" plurals.

Construction: Cut footballs out of construction paper and cut them in half, making sure they are large enough so that you can print a word on each half. On each of four right-hand halves print one of the following plural endings: s, es, ies, ves. All other halves should be used as left-hand halves. On each of these halves print a word that can be made plural by adding s, es, ies, or ves.

Example:

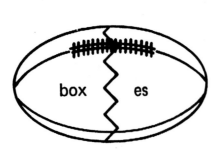
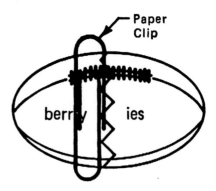

Players: One or two

Materials: Construction paper, marker, paper clips, scissors

Directions: Place the football halves in two piles on a table: the word halves in one pile and the plural endings in the other. The players take turns selecting a word half and matching it with the correct plural half. If the word contains a "y" that should be dropped (as in berry to berries), the player places a paper clip over the "y " in the word.

110: Apple Plurals

Purpose: To provide practice in forming "s," "es," "ies," and "ves" plurals.

Construction: Make thirty apples and four worms out of construction paper. On each apple print the singular form of a word. On each of the four worms, print one of the plural endings: s, es, ies, ves.

Example:

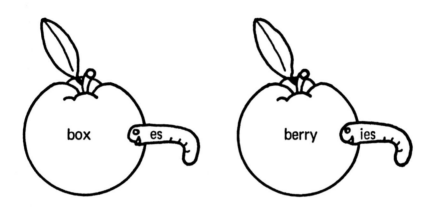

Players: Two to three

Materials: Construction paper, marker, scissors

Directions: Place the apples and worms in two piles on a table. The apples should be together in one pile and the worms in the other. The players take turns selecting an apple and matching it with the correct worm (plural ending). If the word contains a "y" that should be dropped (as in berry to berries), the player will place the worm over the top of the "y" when he forms the plural.

111: Plural Road

Purpose: To provide practice in forming "s," "es," "ies," and "ves" plurals.

Construction: Draw a game board on a large piece of oaktag. Divide the game board into sections, and in each section print a word that can be made plural by adding one of the plural endings (s, es, ies, ves). Arrange the words on the game board so that there is a variety of plural forms. Each player is given a place marker. The markers may be buttons, plastic chips, or any other appropriate object.

Example:

START	box	turkey	berry	knife	fox	monkey	cherry	life	porch
									girl
									lady
	calf	candy	boy	dish	wolf	city	toy	church	thief
	potato								
	frog								
	army	leaf	elf	zero	ax	lace	tree	witch	cave
									wax
END	self	tomato	loaf	patch	kiss	buzz	gas	brush	half

Players: Two to four

Materials: Oaktag, marker, place markers, die

Directions: The players roll the die to determine the number of spaces to be moved for each turn. To stay on a space, the player must read the word and spell its plural form. If he cannot read the word or give its correct plural form, he will go back to a space where he can pronounce the word and give its plural form. Players take turns, and the game continues until one player crosses the finish line. The game board can be changed by printing different words in the spaces.

SYLLABICATION ACTIVITIES

The activities included in this section teach the pupil to recognize one-, two-, three-, four-, five-, and six-syllable words and to apply syllabication rules.

112: Syllable Bird

Purpose: To provide practice in recognizing one-, two-, three-, four-, five-, and six-syllable words.

Construction: Using posterboard, cut out six birdhouses. On each birdhouse draw one, two, three, four, five, or six doors. The number of doors will indicate the number of syllables in a word. Using brightly colored construction paper, cut 24 birds and print a word on each bird. There should be four birds to match each birdhouse: four birds with one-syllable words, four birds with two-syllable words, etc. Place the houses and birds on a large table.

Example:

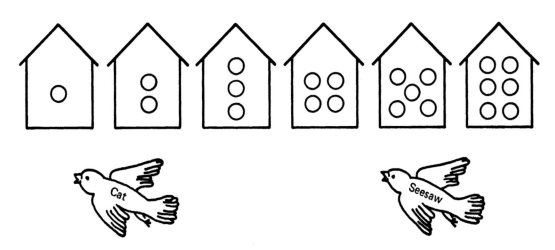

Players: One or two

Materials: Posterboard, construction paper, scissors, marker

Directions: The players will take turns selecting a paper bird, saying the word and identifying the number of syllables in the word, and placing it behind the birdhouse with the appropriate number of doors. The word <u>cat</u> would be placed behind the birdhouse with one door, the word <u>seesaw</u> behind the birdhouse with two doors, etc.

113: Bingo Syllables

Purpose: To provide practice in recognizing one-, two-, three-, four-, five-, and six-syllable words.

Construction: Make bingo cards out of 8″ × 11″ pieces of posterboard. On each bingo card draw five rows and five columns and write a one- to six-syllable word in each square. Use buttons or other small objects for markers.

Players: Two or more

Materials: Posterboard, marker, buttons or other small objects for markers, die

Directions: The teacher will roll a die and call out the number that appears (one to six). Each player will place his marker on a word that contains the same number of syllables as the number that is called. The first player to get five words in a row (across, down, or diagonally) wins the game. A player can place only one marker on his card for each roll of the die.

114: Syllable Match

Purpose: To provide practice in recognizing one-, two-, three-, four-, five-, and six-syllable words.

Construction: On thirty-six 3″ × 5″ index cards, print words that have one to six syllables making six word cards for each number of syllables (one to six). Cut 21 one-inch circles out of construction paper. Use six shoe boxes as containers and cover them with plain Con-Tact paper. Glue the circles to the fronts of the boxes. The boxes will have either one, two, three, four, five, or six circles glued to them. Place the word cards in a pile on a table and also place the shoe boxes on the table. The boxes should be positioned so that the circle side of the box is facing the players

Players: One or two

Materials: Index cards (3″ × 5″), construction paper, scissors, marker, six shoe boxes, clear Con-Tact paper, glue stick

Directions: Each player draws a word card, pronounces the word on the card, and identifies the number of syllables in the word. If he is correct, he will place the card in the shoe box with the correct number of circles on it. The number of circles on the box should correspond with the number of syllables in the word. For example, the word card for <u>bottom</u> would be placed in the box that has two circles on it. Answer cards can be placed in the bottom of the shoe box. At the end of the activity, the players can check the answer key to see how many words were identified correctly.

115: Syllable Fish

Purpose: To provide practice in recognizing one-, two-, three-, four-, five-, and six-syllable words.

Construction: Make fishing rods with small sticks, string, and small magnets. Make numerous fish out of construction paper and on each print a one-, two-, three-, four-, five-, or six-syllable word. Place a paper clip on each fish and spread the fish out on the floor. Make six fishing creels out of oatmeal boxes. Using construction paper, cut out twenty-one large hooks and glue them to the fronts of the fishing creels. Each creel will have either one, two, three, four, five, or six hooks glued to it.

Players: Two to four

Materials: String, four small sticks, four small magnets, construction paper, paper clips, marker, scissors, glue stick, six oatmeal boxes

Directions: Each player will have a fishing rod. Players will take turns trying to hook a fish. If a player catches a fish, he will pronounce the word printed on it, identify the number of syllables in the word, and place the fish in the correct fishing creel. The number of hooks on the fishing creel should correspond with the number of syllables in the word on the fish. Answer keys can be placed in the bottom of each fishing creel. The players can check their answers at the end of each "fishing" game.

116: Syllable Mobile

Purpose: To provide practice in recognizing one-, two-, three-, four-, five-, and six-syllable words.

Construction: Using six different colors of construction paper, cut out numerous 8″ × 3″ strips. Using one strip of each of the six colors, make six syllable identification strips. For example, on one strip of red construction paper print the number "1" and the word DOG, on one strip of green construction paper print the number "2" and the word SUNDAY, etc. The remainder of the strips are left blank. Punch two holes in each of the strips: one hole in the middle at the top and one in the middle at the bottom. Place the blank strips in six piles according to color. Hang the syllable identification strips on a wall in the room. Leave enough room under each of the six strips to hang at least ten more strips.

Example:

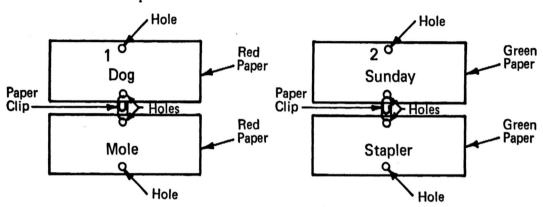

Players: Large group

Materials: Construction paper (six colors), scissors, marker, paper punch, paper clips

Directions: After you have taught the concept of syllabication and practiced identifying one- to six-syllable words, assign the pupils the task of finding sample words for each number of syllables (one to six). The pupils will bring in examples of the words, print them on the appropriate color construction paper and hang them on the mobile. The objective will be to get as many examples as possible for each mobile.

An alternative activity would be to assign each child a particular syllable number (one to six) and have each child make his own mobile seeing who can get the most examples.

117: Syllabication Rule Scoop

Purpose: To provide practice in dividing VCV, VCCV, or Cle words into syllables.

Construction: Cut several ice cream cones out of posterboard. The cones should be at least 4″ high and 3″ wide. Label each cone with one of the three syllabication rules: VCV, VCCV, Cle. Make several cones for each rule. Using various colors of construction paper, cut out circles to represent scoops of ice cream which will fit onto the cones. On each circle print a word which follows one of the syllabication rules printed on the ice cream cones (VCV, VCCV, Cle). Make several words for each rule. Place the ice cream scoops in a pile on a table and place the cones in three piles according to the rules that are printed on them.

Players: One or two

Materials: Posterboard, construction paper, scissors, marker

Directions: The players take turns selecting a scoop of ice cream from the pile, pronouncing the word printed on it, and matching it with the correct ice cream cone. If the player does not match the scoop of ice cream with the correct cone, the ice cream scoop is placed at the bottom of the pile. If the match is correct, the player places the cone with the scoop of ice cream on it in front of him. Play continues until all the scoops of ice cream have been matched with the correct cones. Students may place up to three scoops on the same cone before they must use a new one.

Example:

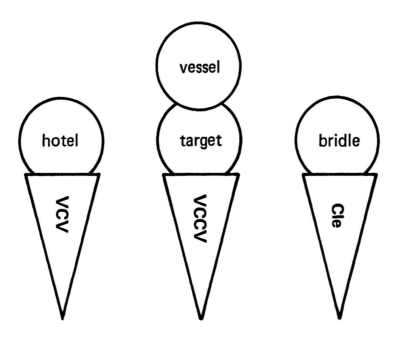

118: Syllabication Rule Apple Tree

Purpose: To provide practice in dividing VCV, VCCV, or Cle words into syllables.

Construction: Take three sheets of posterboard and print one of the rules for dividing words into syllables (VCV, VCCV, Cle) on the bottom of each sheet. Above the rule on each sheet draw the trunk of a tree and an outline for the foliage of the tree. The area where the foliage would appear should occupy the largest part of the paper. Glue several pieces of Velcro to the foliage of the tree. Cut red apples out of construction paper, and on each apple print a multisyllable word that follows one of the syllabication rules (VCV, VCCV, Cle). Make the apples small enough so that several can be placed on each tree. Glue a piece of Velcro to the back of each apple. Hang the three tree posters on a bulletin board and place the apples in a pile on a table near the bulletin board.

Example:

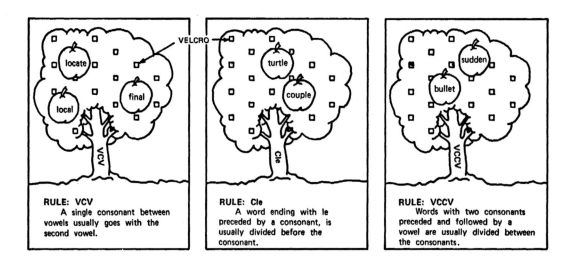

Players: Two to four

Materials: Velcro self-gripping fastener strips, Velcro adhesive, posterboard, red construction paper, scissors, marker

Directions: Players take turns selecting an apple, reading the word on it, identifying what syllabication rule it follows, and attaching it to the appropriate tree (VCV, VCCV, Cle). If a student does not know the word or the rule it follows, he will place the apple at the bottom of the apple pile. To make the activity self-correcting, an answer key can be attached to the back of each posterboard.

119: Syllables on File

Purpose: To provide practice in dividing VCV, VCCV, or Cle words into syllables.

Construction: Print a word that follows the VCV, VCCV, or Cle rule on each of numerous 3″ × 5″ index cards. Leave a slight space between each letter as you print the word. Laminate each of the index cards and place them in a file box.

Players: One

Materials: Index cards (3″ × 5″), laminating material, marker, file box, grease pencil

Directions: The student selects a card and silently reads the word printed on it. He will use the grease pencil to mark where the word should be divided into syllables. To make the activity self-correcting, an answer sheet should be developed.

120: Word Pen

Purpose: To provide practice in dividing into syllables words with a single vowel as a syllable or words with the accent on the first syllable.

Construction: Make thirty piglets out of pink construction paper and write on each of them a word with a single vowel as a syllable (mir a cle, ed u ca tion) or a word with the accent on the first syllable (u′ni verse, i′ so late). Decorate a shoe box to look like a pig pen and print on it the words "Word Pen." Place all the piglets into the "Word Pen."

Players: Two or three

Materials: Pink construction paper, scissors, marker, crayons, a shoe box

Directions: Players take turns picking a piglet from the "Word Pen." After selecting a piglet, the player reads the word and tells how it is divided into syllables. He will also identify the single-vowel syllable or the accented first syllable. If the player is correct, he will keep the piglet. If he is incorrect, he will put the piglet back into the "Word Pen." The player with the most piglets at the end of the game is the winner.

121: Syllable Race

Purpose: To provide practice in dividing into syllables words with a single vowel as a syllable or words with the accent on the first syllable.

Construction: On a large piece of posterboard, draw a zigzag game board and divide it into spaces. Cover the board with clear Con-Tact paper or laminate it. With a grease pencil, print in several spaces a word with a single vowel as a syllable and in several other spaces print a word with the accent on the first syllable (such as above or enough). In the remaining spaces on the game board, print directions such as "Go back two spaces," "Go forward one space," "Lose a turn," or "Take an extra turn." Use buttons or any appropriate small objects for place markers and a die to determine the number of spaces to be moved.

Example:

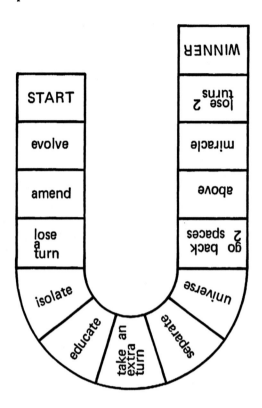

Players: Two or three

Materials: Posterboard, marker, laminating material or clear Con-Tact paper, grease pencil, place markers, die

Directions: Each player takes turns rolling the die and moving the corresponding number of spaces on the game board. In order to stay on a word space, the player must say the word and identify the single vowel syllable or the accented first syllable. If the player is correct, he remains on the space until his next turn. If the player's answer is incorrect, he goes back to the space he occupied before taking his turn. When a player lands on a space that contains a direction, he follows those directions. The first player to reach the finish line is the winner.

The words and directions may be erased after each game, and new words and directions may be printed on the game board to create a different playing board.

122: Skyscraper Syllables

Purpose: To provide practice in dividing into syllables words with a single vowel as a syllable or words with the accent on the first syllable.

Construction: Cut several 8″ × 3″ rectangles out of construction paper. Tack two of the rectangles to the bulletin board so that each will be the top of a vertical column. On the first rectangle print a word that has a single vowel as a syllable (such as mir a cle). On the second rectangle print a word that has the accent on the first syllable (such as i' so late). Place the remainder of the rectangles in a pile on a table near the bulletin board.

Players: Entire class

Materials: Construction paper, scissors, marker, thumbtacks

Directions: Explain to the class how the sample word in each column is divided into syllables. Give the students examples of other words that can be used in each of the columns and have them develop rules for each column. Above each column, print the rule that applies to the words in it. Ask the students to find words that will fit under each of the columns. They will bring the words to class, print them on the blank rectangles, and tack them to the bulletin board under the proper column. The purpose is to make a very high skyscraper. The students can bring in as many words as they can find.

123: Syllable Step-Ups

Purpose: To provide practice in dividing into syllables words with consonant blends or consonant digraphs.

Construction: Print the following guide on the board at the front of the room or on a strip of paper:

> Words that have two consonants in the middle are usually divided between the two consonants.
>
>   vol ley   tim ber
>
> If the two consonants are blends or digraphs, do not divide between the two consonants.
>
>   se <u>cr</u>et   a <u>gr</u>ee

On a piece of posterboard, draw an outline of a staircase with 10 steps. The staircase can be made decorative by coloring it. Using construction paper, cut out 30 strips of paper and print on each strip a two-syllable word that contains a digraph or blend where the word would be divided. Make cartoon-type characters out of construction paper and use them for markers. Each player must have a marker.

Example:

SYLLABLE

STEP UPS

Players: Two or three

Materials: Posterboard, construction paper, scissors, marker, crayons

Directions: The players take turns selecting a word strip, reading the word on it, identifying the blend or digraph, and telling how the word should be divided into syllables. If the player is correct, he can move his marker up one step and he keeps the word strip. If he is incorrect, his marker remains on the same step and the word strip is placed on the bottom of the pile. The first player to reach the top of the staircase is the winner. The activity can be made self-correcting by printing the correct answer on the back of each word strip.

124: Syllabication Exception

Purpose: To provide practice in dividing into syllables words with consonant blends or consonant digraphs.

Construction: Type the following guide at the top of a ditto master:

Words that have two consonants in the middle are usually divided between the two consonants.

   vol ley   tim ber

If the two consonants are blends or digraphs, do not divide between the two consonants.

     se <u>cr</u>et   a <u>gr</u>ee

Below the guide, type directions and a list of words. The directions should instruct the student to mark the blends, digraphs, and double consonants in the words using the following code: blends, BL; digraphs, D; double consonants, DC. After marking the blends, digraphs, and double consonants, the student is to draw a line through the word indicating where the word would be divided into syllables. The list of words should include a variety of examples of blends, digraphs, and double consonants.

Example:

1. re/flect	<u>BL</u>
2. a/gree	<u>BL</u>
3. ath/lete	<u>D</u>
4. cin/der	<u>DC</u>

Players: Entire class

Materials: Ditto master

Directions: Give each student a copy of the worksheet. Review the guide with the students and check to see that they understand it. After reviewing the guide, let the students identify the blends, digraphs, and double consonants in the words, and divide them into syllables. Words that are missed should be retaught so that the students will understand the concept of the rule.

125: Syllabication Bouquet

Purpose: To provide practice in dividing into syllables words with consonant blends or consonant digraphs.

Construction: Using construction paper, cut out 15 daisies, 10 tulips, and 5 roses. Write a two-syllable word containing a consonant blend or digraph on each flower. On the back of each flower, print the proper syllabication of the word. Cut 6 vases out of construction paper making them large enough to hold the flowers. Label 3 vases "Digraphs" and 3 vases "Blends."

Players: Two or three

Materials: Construction paper, scissors, marker

Directions: Each player will be given two vases (one labeled "Digraph" and one labeled "Blend"). The flowers will be scattered word-side up on a table. The players will take turns picking a flower, reading the word on it, and telling how it is divided into syllables. If the player is correct, he will place the flower in one of his vases according to the double consonants contained in it (blend or digraph). If the player is incorrect in any of these tasks, the flower is placed back on the table. The winner is the player who accumulates the largest bouquet of flowers.

126: Picture Affixes

Purpose: To provide practice in dividing into syllables words with affixes.

Construction: Take 3 pictures from magazines or posters and cut each of them into 10 puzzle-like pieces. There must be a puzzle for each player. On each of 30 index cards, print a word with one or two affixes. The picture pieces for each puzzle will be placed in a pile on a table in front of the player. The word cards will be placed face down on the table.

Players: Two or three

Materials: Index cards (3″ × 5″), scissors, marker, magazine pictures or posters

Directions: The players take turns selecting a word card and telling how the word should be divided into syllables. If the player is correct, he keeps the word card and he selects one picture piece for his puzzle. If the player is incorrect, the word card is placed at the bottom of the pile and the player forfeits the opportunity to select a puzzle piece. The player who is the first to complete his picture puzzle wins the game.

127: Affix Cats

Purpose: To provide practice in dividing into syllables words with affixes.

Construction: Cut several large cats from oaktag or heavy paper and laminate them. Cut the cats into three parts—head, middle, and bottom. With a grease pencil, print a root word on the middle part, a prefix on the head, and a suffix on the bottom. Place the pieces on a table in three piles—heads, middles, and bottoms.

Example:

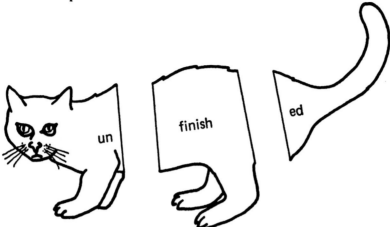

Players: Two or three

Materials: Oaktag or heavy paper, marker, scissors, laminating material, grease pencil

Directions: Players take turns matching the parts of the cats. Each player will select three pieces (head, middle, and bottom) and try to make a word. If he is successful, he keeps the cat. If the three parts do not make a word, the parts are returned to the correct piles. Play continues until all possible combinations have been made. The player with the most cats is the winner.

128: Football Affixes

Purpose: To provide practice in dividing into syllables words with affixes.

Construction: Cut several footballs, football helmets, and football shoes out of different colored construction paper. Cover each of the items with clear Con-Tact. With a grease pencil, print a root word, prefix, or suffix on each of them. Be sure that each item can be matched with at least one other item to form a root word and a prefix, a root word and a suffix, or a root word with a prefix and a suffix. Place all the items face up on a table.

Players: Two or three

Materials: Construction paper, marker, scissors, clear Con-Tact paper, grease pencil

Directions: Players take turns matching the footballs, helmets, and shoes to form words that contain prefixes and/or suffixes. Each player will select either two or three items and attempt to form a word. If he is successful, he will keep the items. If the items do not form a word, the player will place the items back on the table. Play continues until all possible combinations have been made. The player with the most footballs, helmets, and shoes is the winner.

ACTIVITIES TO IMPROVE VOCABULARY AND LITERAL COMPREHENSION

VOCABULARY ACTIVITIES THAT REINFORCE COMPREHENSION

The following activities teach the pupil to pronounce and define vocabulary words, to recognize multiple meaning words, and to correctly pronounce and define technical vocabulary words.

129: Vocabulary Match

Purpose: To provide practice in pronouncing and defining vocabulary words.

Construction: On twenty 3″ × 5″ index cards, print various vocabulary words. On a second set of twenty 3″ × 5″ index cards, make an identical second set of word cards. When you are finished, you will have forty word cards: two cards that contain each of twenty vocabulary words.

Players: Two, four or five

Materials: Forty index cards (3″ × 5″), marker

Directions: Evenly distribute one set of twenty word cards to the players. Place the other set of cards face down in the middle of a table. Each player will take a turn and select a card from the pile. If the card drawn matches a word card in the player's hand, he may keep the match by pronouncing the word and giving its definition. If he can do both tasks correctly, he places the two cards face up on the table in front of him. If the player does not have a match for the card that he draws, the player who does have the matching card has an opportunity to pronounce the word and define it. If he does so correctly, the match is his and he places the two cards face up on the table in front of him. If at any time a player with two matching cards cannot correctly pronounce and define the word, the two cards are placed face down on the table. The winner is the player who makes the most matches (i.e., has the most cards face up on the table in front of him).

At the conclusion of the game, you can check to see which vocabulary words are being missed by checking which cards are placed face down on the table.

130: Definition Football

Purpose: To provide practice in pronouncing and defining vocabulary words.

Construction: On a large piece of posterboard, draw a football field. Include the yard lines and two end zones. Mark the yard lines (10-yard line, 20-yard line, etc.) and place goal posts at either end of the "field." Using posterboard, cut two sets of flashcards: one set cut in the shape of footballs to be used as word cards and one set cut in squares to be used as penalty cards. On each football print a vocabulary word and on each square (penalty card) print a penalty such as "Go back 5 yards," "Go back 10 yards," "Pass intercepted," etc. Place the "football field" on a table and place the football word cards and the penalty cards in two separate piles.

Players: Two or more

Materials: Posterboard, marker, scissors, place markers

Directions: The teacher flips a coin to determine which player (or team) goes first. The players take turns choosing a football word card, pronouncing the word, and giving its definition. If the player is correct, he advances his marker ten yards. If he is incorrect, he chooses a card from the penalty pile and follows the directions printed on it. The winner is the player (or team) that scores the most touchdowns.

131: String a Match

Purpose: To provide practice in defining vocabulary words.

Construction: On both the right and left sides of a large piece of posterboard, attach hooks in a vertical column. Place the hooks far enough apart so that 3″ × 5″ index cards can be placed on each hook. On the right side of each of the hooks in the left-hand column and on the left side of each of the hooks in the right-hand column, insert a brass fastener. Attach a piece of yarn or string to the brass fasteners on the left. The yarn or string should be long enough to reach from the first position on the left column to the last position on the right column. Punch a hole in the middle of several 3″ × 5″ index cards and divide them into two sets. On each card in the first set of cards print a vocabulary word, and on the cards for the other set print the corresponding definition. The activity may be varied so that synonyms, homonyms, or antonyms can also be printed on sets of cards.

Example:

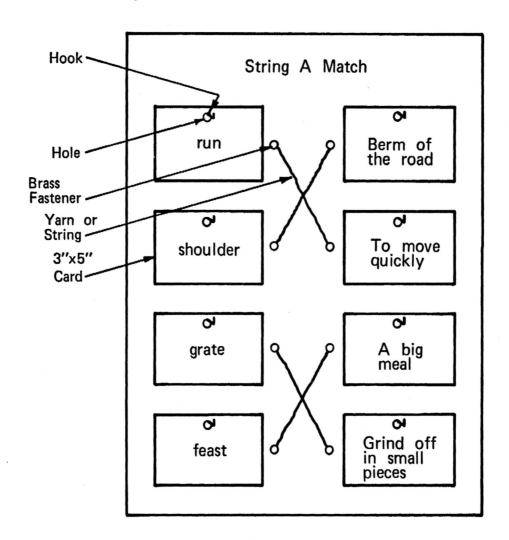

Players: One or two

Materials: Posterboard, paper hooks, brass fasteners, yarn or string, index cards (3″ × 5″), marker

Directions: The children match the words on the left side of the board with the correct definition, synonym, antonym, etc. on the right side. To indicate a match, the yarn or string beside the word in the left-hand column should be attached to the brass fastener beside the correct card in the right-hand column. The activity can be made self-correcting by attaching an answer key to the back of the board.

132: Spin and Define

Purpose: To provide practice in pronouncing and defining vocabulary words.

Construction: Construct a large spinner board from posterboard. Divide the board into ten or more equal parts and laminate it. Using a grease pencil, print a different vocabulary word in each space.

Players: Two or more

Materials: Posterboard, scissors, laminating material, grease pencil

Directions: Students take turns spinning the spinner. They define the word to which the spinner points and use it in a sentence. Each student is awarded one point for each word he can define and use in a sentence correctly. The winner is the student who scores the most points.

133: Multiple Lion

Purpose: To provide practice in recognizing mutliple meaning words in context.

Construction: Prepare a list of words that have mutliple meanings (state, run, grate, etc.) and include with the words their various definitions. Type or print the words and their definitions on a ditto master so that ditto sheets may be distributed to the players. On strips of construction paper, print sentences for each word listed on the vocabulary ditto sheet. Underline the vocabulary word in the sentence. Make three sentence strips for each vocabulary word, making sure that the various definitions of the word are illustrated by the context of the sentence. Place the sentence strips in a pile on a table. Obtain shoe boxes or other types of containers that can hold several sentence strips, and cut a slit in the top of each one. Using construction paper, cut out a lion's head to be pasted to the top of each box. Cut a slit for the lion's mouth, and paste the lion's head to the box, making sure the slit in the lion's head is positioned over the slit already cut in the shoe box. Give each player one of the boxes.

Players: Two

Materials: Ditto master, construction paper, scissors, two shoe boxes, marker

Directions: Review the ditto sheet with the students, making sure they can pronounce and define the multiple meaning words. The students take turns selecting sentence strips from the pile. After selecting a sentence strip and pronouncing the underlined word, the student must define the underlined word as it is used in the sentence. If successful in doing these tasks, the student places the sentence strip in the lion's mouth. If unsuccessful in doing the tasks, the student places the sentence strip on the bottom of the pile. The activity can be made self-correcting by printing the correct definition for the word on the back of each strip.

134: Multiple Meaning Match

Purpose: To provide practice in recognizing multiple meaning words in context.

Construction: Using oaktag strips, print on each a sentence that contains a multiple meaning word. Underline the multiple meaning word in each sentence. Use each multiple meaning word on at least two different strips, making sure that each sentence uses the word in a different way. For example, two sentences for the word <u>grate</u> would be "You will have to <u>grate</u> the cheese for the spaghetti" and "There is a <u>grate</u> in our fireplace." Using additional oaktag strips, print on each a definition for the multiple meaning words. Each definition should correspond to one of the underlined words on the sentence strips. For example, the two definitions for the word <u>grate</u> would be "Rub off in small pieces" and "An iron basket used to contain a fireplace fire." To make the activity self-correcting, place a colored dot or a letter code on the back of each definition strip. Place the same code item on the back of the corresponding sentence strip. Place the sentence strips in a pile on a table and spread the definition strips out face up on the table.

Players: Two

Materials: Oaktag strips, colored pencils, marker, scissors, dictionary

Directions: The players take turns selecting sentence strips from the pile and matching them with the correct definition strips. If the match is correct, the code on the backs of the two strips will be identical. The player will then place both of the strips on the table in front of him. If the match is incorrect, the codes on the backs will not match; the sentence strip will be placed at the bottom of the pile and the definition strip will be placed face up on the table. The winner is the player who gets the most matches. A word that is not known can be checked in the dictionary

135: Multiple Meaning Person

Purpose: To provide practice in recognizing multiple meaning words.

Construction: Using stiff paper, cut out large figures that can be hung in the classroom like mobiles. The figures can be cowboys, skiers, skeletons, etc. On the head of the figure print a multiple meaning word (tire, class, run, state, etc.). You can make a figure for each multiple meaning word you study.

Example:

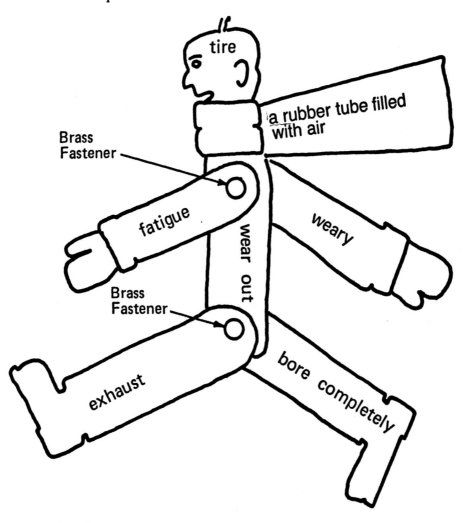

Players: Entire class

Materials: Paper, scissors, marker, dictionary, brass fasteners

Directions: As you study multiple meaning words, you will need to make the students aware of the various meanings a word can have based on the context of the sentence in which it is used. To accomplish this, you can make the figures and print various meanings on the different parts of the body. The figures can be hung in the classroom as a reference point. You might also want the students to make their own figures for assigned words and, using a dictionary, print the various definitions on the figures. The students can then share their work with the class and orally use the multiple meaning word in sentences. The figures made by the students should then be displayed in the classroom.

136: Multiple Meaning Sentences

Purpose: To provide practice in recognizing multiple meaning words.

Construction: On the chalkboard, print a list of words that have multiple meanings (rose, bark, plant, wave, pelt, iron, etc.)

Players: Small or large group

Materials: Chalkboard, chalk, paper, pencils, dictionaries

Directions: Have the students use the dictionaries to discover the different meanings that each word listed on the chalkboard can have. Instruct the students to use the words in sentences—one sentence to illustrate each definition that the multiple meaning word can have. Collect the papers and check the students' sentences. Students who were unable to use the words in sentences to convey the different definitions of the same word will need further study on multiple meaning words.

137: Technical Bulletin Board

Purpose: To provide practice in correctly pronouncing and defining technical vocabulary words.

Construction: Print the new technical vocabulary words to be studied in a lesson on strips of oaktag. Place the word strips in a vertical column on the left-hand side of a bulletin board. Leave space to the right of each word for three more columns. In the first and second columns, attach card pockets directly opposite the vocabulary words. In the first pocket, place slips of paper with the page number(s) where the word appears in the lesson. This will enable the pupils to take the slips back to their desks as they work on the word. In the second pocket, place a slip of paper with the correct definition for the word. The third column will be used when you are teaching the word in the lesson. After the students have defined each of the words, print the definition on a strip of oaktag and place it in the third column.

Example:

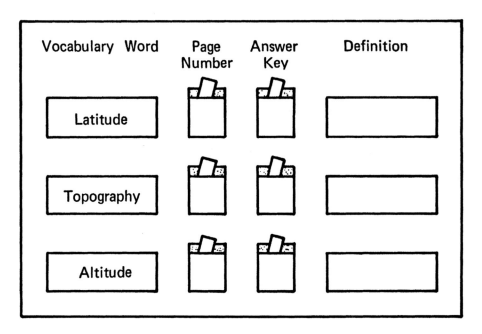

Players: Entire class

Materials: Oaktag strips, marker, scissors, card pockets, thumbtacks, paper

Directions: The students will use the bulletin board as a learning center. A few days before the lesson is to be introduced, place the new technical vocabulary words on the bulletin board. Place the slips of paper with the appropriate page number(s) and the definition in the pockets. When the student has time for independent work, he will come up to the bulletin board, copy the vocabulary word, and take a slip that tells the lesson page(s) where the word is found. The student will return to his desk, read the appropriate page(s), and write his definition for each new vocabulary word. To check the definitions, he will go up to the bulletin board and check the answer printed on the answer key in the pocket.

This activity should be used as a learning center. When you are ready to use the word in the lesson, have one of the pupils read the sentence from the lesson in which the word appears and orally give its definition. He will then print the definition on an oaktag strip and place it in the last column to the right of the word. After the definitions are placed in the correct position on the bulletin board, the pupils can refer to them when they are studying the lesson. The bulletin board will help introduce the new words and also serve as a visual means of reviewing the words.

138: Team Technical Match

Purpose: To provide practice in correctly pronouncing and defining technical vocabulary words.

Construction: Print the definitions for several technical vocabulary words on the chalkboard. Print the technical vocabulary words and the sentence from the lesson in which they appear on large oaktag strips. Underline the vocabulary word in each sentence.

Players: Two teams with an equal number of players

Materials: Chalkboard, chalk, oaktag strips, marker

Directions: Divide the students into two equal teams. Hold up the sentence cards for the vocabulary words one at a time and select a student to pronounce the word and read the sentence as it appears on the strip. Alternate which teams and players have an opportunity to answer. If the player correctly reads the sentence, he will then identify from the definitions on the chalkboard the correct definition for the technical vocabulary word. If he does this correctly, the student's team scores one point. If his answer is incorrect, no points are scored and the sentence strip is placed on the bottom of the pile. The team scoring the most points is the winner.

139: Technical Match-Up

Purpose: To provide practice in correctly pronouncing and defining technical vocabulary words.

Construction: Using strips of oaktag, print a technical vocabulary word on the left and a definition for the word on the right. Cut the strips in half by cutting a jagged edge between the two halves of the strip. Place the two halves in two separate piles. Place the definition halves face up on a table and the word halves in a pile near them.

Players: Two

Materials: Oaktag strips, marker, scissors

Directions: Students alternate turns selecting word strips from the pile and pronouncing the word orally. If the student can correctly pronounce the word, he attempts to match it with the correct definition strip. If the student correctly matches the word half with the definition half, he keeps the two halves. If he cannot pronounce the word or match it to the correct defintion, the word strip is placed on the bottom of the pile. The winner is the player who correctly matches the most strips.

140: The Technical Car

Purpose: To provide practice in recognizing technical vocabulary words.

Construction: Using oaktag or other stiff paper, cut out a large car. Cut the car into sections (wheels, fenders, door, hood, etc.). Reassemble the car's parts by attaching them to a chalkboard or bulletin board. Draw horizontal lines on the board. The lines will be used to print the letters that spell a technical vocabulary word. The number of lines drawn will correspond to the number of letters contained in the technical vocabulary word. The words that are to be used in the activity may be listed on the board in random order.

Players: Small group

Materials: Chalkboard, chalk, oaktag, scissors, crayons or colored pencils

Directions: Students take turns guessing a letter that they believe is in the technical vocabulary word that is being spelled. If a correct letter is named, you print the letter on the appropriate line. If a letter named is incorrect, you remove one of the parts of the car. The object of the activity is to spell the word before the car is disassembled. The car is completely reassembled before you begin a new word.

LITERAL COMPREHENSION ACTIVITIES THAT DEVELOP UNDERSTANDING

Activities in the remainder of this section teach the pupils to answer factual questions, to follow directions, to sequence ideas read, and to select important details from materials read.

141: Factual Review

Purpose: To provide practice in answering factual questions.

Construction: To review a unit in a reader, prepare questions from stories in the unit. The questions and their answers should be familiar to the students. Print each question on a small strip of oaktag and place them all in a box. On a large piece of posterboard, draw a line down the middle to divide the board into two sections. On the left side print the titles of stories in the unit. On the right side and opposite each title, glue a library card pocket.

Example:

STORY TITLE	FACTUAL QUESTIONS
Red Fox	
Adventureland	
Cowboy Mike	

Players: Small group

Materials: Posterboard (8″ × 11″), library card pockets, glue, marker, paper, a box

Directions: Each student takes a turn and selects a question strip from the box. He reads the question orally, gives the answer, and matches it to the correct story title. If he is correct, the strip is placed in the pocket beside the story title and the student is awarded one point. If his answer is incorrect, the strip is returned to the box. The winner is the player who has the most points (i.e., the player who places the most strips in the correct pockets). The strips can be color coded on the back to make the activity self-correcting.

142: Factual Pictures

Purpose: To provide practice in answering factual questions.

Construction: Cut out descriptive pictures from magazines, newspapers, etc. Paste them to stiff paper and place them in an envelope. On strips of paper, write sentences that describe the pictures.

Example:

Picture: Picture of a quarterback throwing a touchdown pass to his end.

Sentence: "The opposing team's defense could not stop the end from scoring a touchdown."

Spread the sentence strips out on a table. Color code the backs of both the pictures and the sentence strips so that the student can check his answers.

Players: One or two

Materials: Pictures from magazines, newspapers, etc., stiff paper, scissors, marker or pen, paper, envelope, paste

Directions: Players take turns selecting a picture from the envelope and matching it with the correct sentence strip. If the player is correct, he places the picture on top of the sentence strip and places them on the table in front of him. If he is incorrect, the sentence strip is returned to the table and the picture is placed back into the envelope.

143: Factual Spinner

Purpose: To provide practice in answering factual questions.

Construction: Make a wheel-shaped board out of oaktag and divide it into sections. Print questions on small strips of paper and, using paper clips or other fasteners, attach one strip to each section of the wheel. The questions should be from stories that the students have studied. The titles of the stories can be printed on a sheet of paper that can be used by the students as an aid to remembering the stories. Attach a spinner to the middle of the wheel.

Players: Two

Materials: Oaktag, brass fasteners, marker, paper

Directions: The students take turns spinning the spinner, answering the question, and identifying the story where the answer appeared. If a student answers correctly and identifies the correct story, he is awarded one point. The winner is the student who scores the most points. At the conclusion of each game, the questions on the board should be changed.

144: Factual Identification

Purpose: To provide practice in answering factual questions.

Construction: On a ditto master, type quotations from the dialogue between characters in a story that the students have previously read. Type the names of the characters at the bottom of the sheet.

Players: Entire class

Materials: Ditto master

Directions: The students read each quotation on the ditto sheet and match it with the name of the character who made the statement. The exercise can be varied by using different types of questions (places, important events, etc.) rather than quotations.

145: Picture Directions

Purpose: To provide practice in correctly following directions.

Construction: On a ditto master, draw several pictures arranged in a predetermined sequence (draw three pictures horizontally and three pictures vertically, etc.). Written directions such as the following should accompany the drawings.

1. Draw a circle around the house.
2. Connect the tree and the bird with a dotted line.
3. Put an X over the person.

Example:

Players: One or more

Materials: Ditto master

Directions: The student reads the directions on the ditto sheet and performs the indicated tasks. You may also make a learning center with this idea. Follow all the directions listed above, but cut pictures out of magazines and glue them to a piece of posterboard. Print the directions at the top of the posterboard. To make the learning center reusable, laminate the board or cover it with clear Con-Tact paper and have the student use a grease pencil. Letters, numbers, or other symbols may also be substituted for the pictures.

146: Directional Objects

Purpose: To provide practice in correctly following directions.

Construction: Collect numerous beads and small objects of various shapes and place them in a small box. On index cards, print directions about assembling the objects in a certain order.

Example:

1. Place an oblong bead to the right of a small button.
2. Place a paper clip to the left of the button.
3. Move the button to the left of the paper clip and place the bead so that it touches the paper clip's right side.

On the back of the index card, draw a diagram showing how the objects should be placed when the final direction has been executed. Place the index cards with the directions printed on them in a pile on a table and place the box of objects beside the cards.

Players: Two or more

Materials: Index cards ($3'' \times 5''$), a small box, beads, buttons, paper clips, and various other small objects, marker

Directions: Students take turns selecting an index card and following the directions printed on it. If the directions are followed correctly, the student scores one point. If the directions are not followed correctly, no points are scored. When a student has completed following the directions, whether or not he has been successful, all objects are returned to the box and the card is placed on the bottom of the pile. The winner is the student who scores the most points.

147: Scavenger Directions

Purpose: To provide practice in correctly following directions.

Construction: When the students are not in the classroom, hide various objects around the room. On several index cards, write directions for finding each object. Use four or more cards to give the complete directions for each object's hiding place.

Example:

Card 1	1. Start at the teacher's desk.
	2. Walk three steps toward the back of the room.
Card 2	1. Turn 90° left.
	2. Walk two steps in this direction.
Card 3	1. Turn 90° right.
	2. Walk four steps toward the back of the room.

Card 4
1. Place your hand on the fourth shelf of the bookcase.
2. Find the fifth book from the right on the shelf and open it to page 30.
3. Take out the leaf placed on this page.

Place the cards on a table at the front of the room. Group or color code the sets of cards for each object and place the cards together. Directions for finding the leaf are printed on pink cards, directions for finding the button are printed on green cards, etc.

Players: Entire class or small group

Materials: Index cards (3″ × 5″), assorted objects (buttons, leaves, pictures, shoe strings, etc.), marker

Directions: Divide the class into teams (two or more) and have each team designate one student as a "direction follower." The players on each team take turns selecting a card and reading it aloud to the "direction follower." The directions may be read only once. If the "direction follower" cannot follow the directions, he returns to the starting point and the exercise is begun again. If he successfully follows the directions and finds the object, he gives the object to a member of his team to hold. The team then selects another set of direction cards and attempts to find another object. The winning team is the one that finds the most objects. The cards for the objects that have been found are returned to the table.

148: Follow That Direction

Purpose: To provide practice in correctly following directions.

Construction: Supply each child with a blank sheet of paper and a pencil. On index cards, write directions for a designated task.

Example:

1. Print the number 4 on the top line at the left of your paper.
2. Print a 5 on the second line and print it directly below the 4.
3. Print an 8 to the right side of the 5.
4. Print a 6 on the third line and print it directly below the 5.
5. Print a 7 on the fourth line and print it directly below the 6.
6. To the left of the 7, print a 2 and then a 3. The 2 should be beside the 7 and the 3 should be beside the 2.
7. Print a 10 on the fifth line and print it directly below the 7.
8. To the right of the 10 on the fifth line print these numbers in this order: 1,4,8.

The exercise can end here or you can continue it by printing additional directions on the cards such as the following:

1. Draw a straight line and connect the two 4's.
2. Draw a straight line and connect the two 8's.
3. Draw a square around the 5.
4. Draw an X over the 6.
5. Draw a triangle around the numbers 2,7,10.
6. Draw a circle around the 3.
7. Leave the 1 as it is. Do not draw a circle around it.

Example:

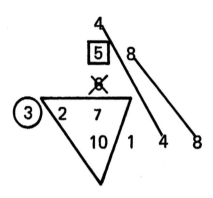

Players: Entire class or small group

Materials: Index cards (3″ × 5″), paper, pencils

Directions: Read the directions orally to the group. Read each direction very clearly and watch to see if the children are able to execute the direction. Read each direction only once. Children who cannot follow long and involved directions will have to have easier directions to follow. You may check the papers at the end of the exercise, or you may print the answer on the chalkboard and have each student check his own paper. The directions may also be given to the children to read and follow. The answer may be printed on the back of one of the index cards.

149: Sequential Sentences

Purpose: To provide practice in sequencing events.

Construction: On several strips of oaktag, print sentences from a short paragraph that has been previously read by the student. Print one sentence per strip of oaktag. Scramble the sentence strips and place them together on a table.

Players: One

Materials: Oaktag strips, marker

Directions: The child places the sentence strips in the correct sequential order. When the child has placed the sentences in the order that he believes to be correct, he reads the paragraph aloud. The exercise can be made self-correcting by marking the backs of the strips according to the correct sequence.

150: Eventual Sequence

Purpose: To provide practice in sequencing events.

Construction: Cut out of magazines or books pictures that illustrate the beginning of a sequence of events (auto accident, house on fire, fish being caught, etc.). Mount the pictures on oaktag and laminate them or cover them with clear Con-Tact paper. Place them in a box or other holder.

Players: One, small group, or entire class

Materials: Pictures from magazines and books, oaktag, laminating materials or clear Con-Tact paper, a box

Directions: The student selects a picture card and lists in sequential order the events that would occur as a result of the event illustrated in the picture.

Example:

Picture—Fish being caught by a fisherman. Child lists the following:
1. reel it in
2. land it
3. take the hook out of the fish
4. place the fish on a stringer
5. clean the fish
6. cook the fish
7. eat the fish

To make the activity self-correcting, suggested sequential steps can be listed on the back of the picture card. However, because of the nature of this activity, you should check the individual responses. The activity can be used as a class activity by showing the picture to the class and having them give the sequence of events.

151: Sequential Symbols

Purpose: To provide practice in sequencing events.

Construction: Using oaktag strips, print incomplete activity sequences. The sequences may be numbers, letters, designs, etc. Laminate the strips or cover them with clear Con-Tact paper.

Example:
1. 1—11—111—
2. AA—BB—CC—
3. 121—232—343—
4. AZ—BY—CX—

Players: One or small group

Materials: Oaktag strips, marker, laminating materials or clear Con-Tact paper

Directions: The student selects a card and copies the sequence printed on the card onto his paper. He then writes the next two combinations in the sequence.

152: Cartoon Sequence

Purpose: To provide practice in sequencing events.

Construction: Obtain comic strips from the newspaper or from comic books. Select frames that show an obvious sequence of events and mount them on stiff paper. Cut the frames apart and place them in an envelope. Place each sequence in a separate envelope. Prepare several comic strip sequences in this manner.

Players: One or small group

Materials: Comic strips from newspapers or comic books, scissors, stiff paper, glue stick, envelopes

Directions: The students select an envelope and place the comic strip frames on their table or desks. They place the frames in the proper sequence according to the events depicted. By numbering the backs of the frames, the activity can be made self-correcting.

153: Detail Challenge

Purpose: To provide practice in selecting details.

Construction: After reading a story in the basal reader, write a number of questions that ask the child to select details from the story. Use questions such as "Where was the car going?", "Who was driving the car?", "How much money was stolen?", etc. Print the questions on strips of construction paper and place them in a shoe box. Print the number "1" on a 5″ × 8″ index card and make similar cards for the numbers "2," "3," and "4." These will be the point value cards and should be placed face down on your desk.

Players: Small group

Materials: Four index cards (5″ × 8″), construction paper strips, one shoe box, chalk, pen

Directions: Divide the group into two equal teams. Members of each team will take turns, and each team will alternate answering the questions. You will determine the point value of each question by selecting one of the four 5″ × 8″ index cards numbered "1" to "4." A point value card will be drawn before each question strip is selected. Select a question strip from the shoe box and read the question to the appropriate team member. If the question is answered correctly, the player's team will earn the number of points determined by the point value card previously drawn. If the question is not answered correctly, no points are given to the team and the player whose turn it is on the opposite team has a chance to answer the question. If his answer is correct, his team is awarded the point(s). If his answer is not correct, no points are awarded to either team. On the chalkboard, record each team's score, or appoint a scorekeeper. The game continues until all the question strips in the shoe box have been used. The winner is the team that scores the most points.

154: Detail Cards

Purpose: To provide practice in selecting details.

Construction: On a ditto master, type or print detail phrases from a story that was previously read by the pupils. Leave a blank space in front of each phrase. On 5″ × 8″ index cards, print questions that can be answered by one of the phrases on the ditto. Each question is assigned a number that is printed in the upper right-hand corner of the card.

Example:

Students' Ditto Sheet

_____ in the wicker basket

Question Card

Where was the dog hiding?   1

Players: Entire class or small group

Materials: Ditto master, index cards (5″ × 8″)

Directions: Distribute a ditto sheet to each student who is participating in the activity. Select a question card, read the number in the upper right-hand corner and then read the question aloud. The student will print the question number beside the correct detail phrase on his ditto sheet. When the exercise is completed, collect the papers and check the student responses. Students who have difficulty with the exercise will need more practice with details.

155: Personality Details

Purpose: To provide practice in selecting details.

Construction: Select names of well-known people from history, sports, politics, medicine, science, space explorations, current events, movies and television. etc. Print their names in a vertical column on the chalkboard. On a sheet of paper or on 3″ × 5″ index cards, print details that can serve as key points for identifying the person.

Examples:

John F. Kennedy
1. Hero of PT 109
2. President of USA
3. Assassinated in Dallas

Franco Harris
1. Plays for the Pittsburgh Steelers
2. Wears Number 32
3. Third leading rusher in NFL history

Players: Entire class or small group

Materials: Paper or index cards (3″ × 5″), chalkboard, chalk, pen

Directions: Divide the group into two equal teams. The members of each team will take turns, and each team will alternate answering. Read the description of one of the personalities to the group. The student whose turn it is to answer will identify one of the names listed on the chalkboard. If his answer is correct, his team will be awarded one point. If his answer is incorrect, no point is awarded and you will proceed to another description. Those descriptions that are not correctly identified can be used again at a later time in the game. The winner is the team that scores the most points.

Section 5

ACTIVITIES TO IMPROVE INTERPRETIVE COMPREHENSION AND CRITICAL READING

ACTIVITIES THAT IMPROVE INTERPRETIVE READING SKILLS

The following activities provide practice in identifying main ideas not explicitly stated, drawing and predicting logical conclusions, interpreting key concepts about story characters, and associating the text with the correct pictures. Additional activities are provided in the areas of following plot sequence, classifying information under appropriate categories, determining cause-and-effect relationships, and summarizing material read.

156: Main Idea Travel Brochure

Purpose: To provide practice in identifying main ideas not explicitly stated.

Construction: You and/or the children bring to class copies of ads from travel brochures or the travel sections of newspapers. Descriptions of places such as Disneyland, the Grand Canyon, Gettysburg, Indianapolis, Williamsburg, etc. can be used. Bring in enough different brochures or newspapers so that each child in the group will have two from which to choose. From the two brochures or newspaper sections, each child will select one place that he wants to advertise. He will select from his brochure or newspaper four or five sentences that he believes convey the main idea of the place being advertised. He writes the sentences on a 3″ × 5″ index card and prints the name of the place being advertised on the back of the card. Check the completed cards to be sure they contain enough information to allow other children to guess the name of the advertised place.

Before you begin this activity, you will need to teach the concept of main idea and do one or two travel ads with the group.

Example:

Come to historic Pennsylvania and visit this famous battlefield. On this battlefield occurred one of the most decisive battles of American and of world history. President Lincoln delivered one of his most famous speeches here. Here also is the residence of the late President Dwight D. Eisenhower.

(Gettysburg)

Players: Small group

Materials: Index cards (3″ × 5″), travel brochures and/or newspaper travel sections

Directions: Each child reads his advertisement to the group. The children in the group attempt to name the place described. If the group has difficulty with the activity, the names of the places being described should be listed in random order on the chalkboard.

157: Main Idea Paragraphs

Purpose: To provide practice in identifying main ideas not explicitly stated.

Construction: Cut selected short descriptive paragraphs from magazines, *Weekly Readers*, children's magazines, etc. Mount them on oaktag squares. Leave room below each paragraph to print three suggested titles for the paragraph. Cover the oaktag squares with clear Con-Tact paper or laminate them.

Example:

It was slip and slide today as the first heavy snowfall of the winter season fell on the city. Most motorists were stranded by the surprise snowfall and spent many hours attempting to drive home. To try to ease the traffic congestion that resulted, salt trucks and their crews were called out.

From the titles listed below, select the one that is best for the paragraph.

1. The Beginning of Winter
2. Police and Stranded Drivers
3. The Weatherman Saves the Day

Players: Two or small group

Materials: Oaktag squares; grease pencils; newspapers, *Weekly Readers*, children's magazines, etc.; clear Con-Tact paper or laminating materials

Directions: Distribute three or more oaktag squares to each child in the group. The children will silently read the paragraphs on them and circle one of the titles listed. After the children complete this task, they will take turns reading the paragraphs aloud and identifying the titles they selected. The other children in the group will decide if the title selected is the best one. If the group believes a different title is better, they as well as the reader will have to defend their decisions. You will help them decide which title is the most appropriate.

The exercise may also be played by two players. The players take turns reading the paragraph aloud and deciding which title is best. If the reader is correct, he will receive one point. If his answer is incorrect, the other player may receive the point by identifying the correct title. The activity may be made self-correcting by assigning each card a number and listing the numbers and the correct titles on an answer key.

158: Main Idea Pictures

Purpose: To provide practice in identifying main ideas not explicitly stated.

Construction: Cut several pictures from magazines and mount them on individual sheets of oaktag. Select pictures depicting a scene or an action that can be titled (such as a man landing a large fish, a lady walking through deep snow without boots, or a sailboat on the ocean). Laminate the pictures or cover them with clear Con-Tact paper.

Players: Entire class or small group

Materials: Oaktag, magazines, clear Con-Tact paper or laminating materials, paper, pencils

Directions: Distribute one or two pictures to each student in the group. The student will study the picture(s) and write on his sheet of paper what he believes would be a suitable title for the picture(s). Collect the pictures from the students and place them on the chalk tray, bulletin board, or another place where they can be easily viewed by the group. Each child will then read his title(s) aloud to the group and they will try to guess which picture each title identifies. A winner can be determined by seeing which student identifies the most correct pictures.

This exercise should be used when you are first introducing the concept of identifying main ideas not explicitly stated.

159: Contextual Conclusions

Purpose: To provide practice in drawing logical conclusions.

Construction: On ditto masters, type short paragraphs that require the student to draw logical conclusions based on the material given in the paragraph. The paragraphs may be created by you or taken from materials that have been studied in class.

Example:

The sky was gray. The ground was white. It was a cold December day. The children were excited. They were going to grandmother's house to celebrate _____.

   a. Christmas
   b. Thanksgiving
   c. Memorial Day

The general was tired. He had fought all day. His blue uniform was tattered and torn. He did not like to fight against the Southern soldiers. This war sometimes caused brothers to fight against brothers. It was the _____ War.

a. Revolutionary
b. Civil
c. French and Indian

Players: Entire class

Materials: Typewriter, ditto masters, pencils

Directions: Distribute a ditto sheet to each pupil in the class. The children will select the correct word to complete each paragraph. When the children have written the answers, collect the papers and check the exercise. Children who have missed some of the answers will need further practice and instruction.

160: Questionable Conclusion

Purpose: To provide practice in drawing logical conclusions.

Construction: Using oaktag, cut out squares large enough to hold a paragraph and a question that requires the student to draw a logical conclusion based on the material read in the paragraph. You may create the paragraph yourself and print it on the oaktag card, or cut paragraphs out of newspapers, magazines, Weekly Readers, etc. and mount them on the cards. Print the correct answer to the question on the back of each card. Laminate the cards or cover them with clear Con-Tact paper. Place the cards in a large envelope or folder.

Example:

John, a nine-year-old boy, was standing on a hill that overlooked a deserted highway. As he looked down from the hill, he saw two cars collide. He was the only person who saw the accident. He was the only one who could help the injured people.

What should John do?

1. Run down from the hill and direct traffic
2. Sit on the hill and watch the people
3 Run for help

Players: One or two

Materials: Oaktag; scissors; magazines, newspapers, Weekly Readers, etc.; glue stick; marker; grease pencil; large envelope or folder; laminating materials or clear Con-Tact paper

Directions: The student selects a card, reads the paragraph, and circles the correct answer. Students may check their answers by referring to the backs of the cards. If the answer is correct, the student will place the card on his right side. If the answer is incorrect, the student will place the card on his left side. When all the cards are completed, the pupil will raise his hand and you can review with him the ones he missed.

161: Animal Print Conclusions

Purpose: To provide practice in drawing logical conclusions.

Construction: After the class has studied or read about animals and their habits, draw sets of their footprints on the chalkboard. Number each set of prints and write the animal's name beside the prints.

Example:

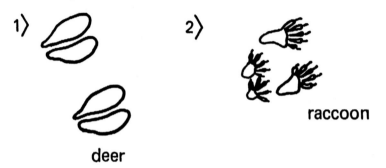

1)

2)

raccoon

deer

On 3″ × 5″ index cards write descriptive sentences about each of the animals. The sentences can be about the animal's habits, appearance, food, enemies, home, etc.

Example:

The card for "raccoon" would read as follows:
1. He looks like a bandit
2. He likes to raid garbage cans.
3. He has a bushy tail.

Players: Entire class

Materials: Index cards (3″ × 5″), chalkboard, chalk

Directions: Place the description cards on your desk. Draw a card, read the descriptive sentences, and have the children volunteer to answer. The student must look at the chalkboard, give the number beside the correct animal's prints, and give the name of the animal. Each child should be given an opportunity to answer at least one question.

162: Prediction Papers

Purpose: To provide practice in predicting logical outcomes.

Construction: Plan a special activity for the class that will lend itself to the process of predicting the logical outcome of a series of events. Before the special activity is undertaken with the class, discuss with them what the possible outcome might be. Examples would be the planting of a seed in a container, a trip to a zoo, tadpoles placed in an aquarium, etc. After the discussion has taken place, distribute a piece of paper and a pencil to each child.

Players: Entire class

Materials: Paper, pencils, materials for the classroom activity (tadpoles, aquarium, seed, container, etc.), large envelope

Directions: Following a brief discussion about the activity and possible outcomes, the children will write what they believe will be the outcome. The predictions are to be as complete as possible and, when appropriate, written in sequential order of occurrence (tadpoles to frogs). The paper is signed by the student and all papers are collected and placed in a large envelope. When the activity has progressed to the point where the outcome can be seen (tadpoles turn into frogs), the predictions that were written by the students are retrieved from the envelope, and the predictions are compared to the actual outcome.

163: Predicting in the Content Areas

Purpose: To provide practice in predicting logical outcomes.

Construction: Use the student's science book of experiments, a history book, or a geography book to plan a lesson based on predicting outcomes.

Example:

Science
1. Experiments
2. Food chains
3. Events that affect the lives of animals or insects

History
1. Wars
2. Political elections
3. Exploration of new areas or worlds
4. New trade routes

Geography
1. Industry that a country would have
2. Clothing people might wear
3. Building materials used for homes

Players: Entire class

Materials: Paper, pencils, content subject books

Directions: When you are studying an event in the content subject areas of history or geography or conducting an experiment in science, read and discuss the material without exposing the outcome to the class. When you believe the students have enough information to predict what will happen, have them write their predictions on a sheet of paper. Read the concluding information in the history or geography book or conduct the science experiment. After the outcome has been learned, have the students compare the results with their predictions. If their predicted outcomes did not occur, discuss why they think it did not happen as they predicted.

164: Weatherman

Purpose: To provide practice in predicting logical outcomes.

Construction: Write or phone the local weather agency and obtain from them weather tables for the previous year or two. Books that discuss the weather and related topics (such as wind currents, barometric readings, jet stream, etc.) should be obtained from the library. Contact a local weatherman or agency to see if someone will come to your classroom to discuss weather prediction with the class.

Players: Entire class

Materials: Reference books on weather, paper, pencils, speaker from a local weather agency

Directions: Develop a unit on weather with the students. As part of the unit, discuss the job of the weatherman and why he performs an important service (long-range forecasts may allow people to evacuate before a tidal wave hits, traffic jams are avoided in a snow storm, damage to crops by frost may be avoided, etc.). In the unit, study how a weatherman predicts the weather and discuss the instruments and tools of his trade (wind gauge, barometer, rain gauge, etc.). A local weatherman may be called in as a speaker after his job and tools have been studied.

Activities that can be done in conjunction with this unit are as follows:

1. Keeping charts on rainfall
2. Student weathermen who predict the next day's weather
3. Tabulating how often a weatherman is correct in his prediction
4. Have students do long-range predictions for holidays.

Students will enjoy predicting the weather and learning how the weatherman prepares his daily forecast.

165: Guess the Character

Purpose: To provide practice in interpreting key concepts about story characters.

Construction: On the chalkboard print a list of popular characters who are familiar to the students, such as Tony the Tiger, Jolly Green Giant, Ronald McDonald, Pillsbury Doughboy, Fred Flintstone, Superman, the Hulk, etc. You may also want to include historical characters and characters from stories in the students' readers. Assign a number to each character's name. On separate 3″ × 5″ index cards write key concepts about each character.

Players: Entire class

Materials: Chalkboard, chalk, index cards (3″ × 5″), pen

Directions: Select a character description card from the pile and read it aloud to the class. Students will volunteer to identify the character being described. The class decides whether or not the answer is correct and discusses the reason it is an appropriate answer.

A variation of the activity would be to read want ads for the characters and have the students decide which character could fit the ad.

Example:

> Wanted: One giant green man. Must live in a valley and harvest vegetables. Must have good voice for saying "Ho! Ho! Ho!"
>
> (Jolly Green Giant)

166: Character Hold-Up

Purpose: To provide practice in interpreting key concepts about story characters.

Construction: On 3″ × 5″ index cards print the names of characters from stories the children have read in their readers. Make duplicate cards so that each student in the class will have a set of cards representing all the characters to be used in this activity. Prepare a short descriptive paragraph for each character and print them on separate 3″ × 5″ index cards.

Players: Entire class

Materials: Index cards (3″ × 5″), marker

Directions: Distribute the character cards to the children so that all children are holding a card for each character. Select a card from the character description cards and read it aloud to the class. When you have read the description, each child will hold up the index card that he believes contains the name of the character described. The children should be encouraged to discuss why they believe their answer is correct.

167: Hang a Character

Purpose: To provide practice in interpreting key concepts about story characters.

Construction: Select from magazines, books, newspapers, etc. pictures of well-known personalities from sports, movies, current events, etc. as well as characters from stories in basal readers. Mount the pictures on 5″ × 8″ index cards, cover them with clear Con-Tact paper, and punch a hole in the middle of the top of the card. On another set of index cards, print key concepts about each of the characters pictured. Cover these cards with clear Con-Tact paper and punch a hole in the middle of the top of each card. Using a large piece of posterboard, attach and space Christmas tree ornament hooks in rows and columns. Push one end of the hook through the posterboard and place masking tape over it. Hang a picture card on each hook. Place the character concept cards in a pile on a table.

Example:

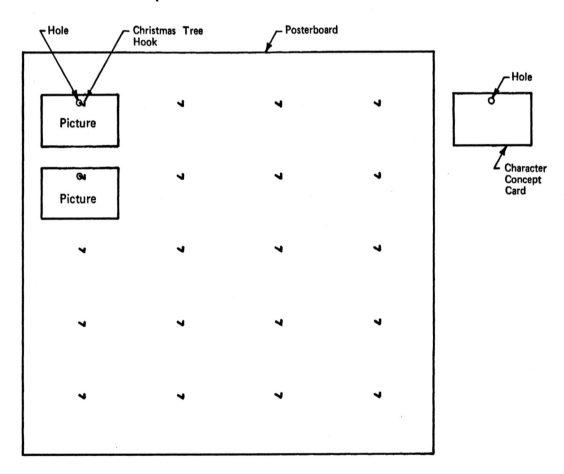

Players: Two

Materials: Large sheet of posterboard, marker, clear Con-Tact paper, index cards (5″ × 8″), paper punch, Christmas tree ornament hooks, masking tape

Directions: Players alternate turns selecting character description cards. If the student knows which character is being described, he hangs the card over the picture. If the student cannot match the description card to the correct picture, the description card is placed at the bottom of the pile. The winner of the activity is the student who matches the most pictures and descriptions. The exercise can be made self-correcting by placing numbers on the backs of the cards so that cards that match will have the same number.

168: Camera Creations

Purpose: To provide practice in associating the text with the correct pictures.

Construction: Organize a trip to a zoo, fire station, museum, arboretum, historic site, nature preserve, etc. Take along a camera and take snapshots of the important sights observed. Have the film developed and bring the snapshots to class for the students to see.

Players: Entire class

Materials: Camera, film, pencils, crayons, writing paper, large envelopes

Directions: Share each snapshot with the class and encourage the students to discuss them in detail. After each picture is discussed, attach it with masking tape to the chalkboard. Follow this procedure with each picture that was taken. When all the pictures have been discussed, direct the students to select one picture and write a descriptive paragraph about it. When the paragraphs are completed, the students can volunteer to read their paragraphs to the class. When the exercise is completed, place all the paragraphs for each picture in large envelopes and paste the picture to the front of the envelope. Place the envelopes in the classroom reading corner so that the students can read the paragraphs during their free time.

    A variation of the activity would be to use snapshots of the students as they are engaged in school activities (school plays, talent shows, lunch hour, gym, recess, music lessons, getting on or off the school bus, the principal's office, etc.).

169: Question the Picture

Purpose: To provide practice in associating the text with the correct pictures.

Construction: Use a history or geography book or a basal reader for this activity.

Players: Entire class

Materials: History book, geography book, or basal reader

Directions: When a new unit or chapter is introduced to the class, teach the students to preview the lesson before beginning to read. Part of the preview step would include discussion of the pictures that are contained on each of the pages to be read. Direct the students to study the pictures and decide what they believe will be happening in the written text on that page. Students should discuss the pictures to establish questions that they want to answer. After the discussion, students should read the written text to find the answers to their questions. The procedure of studying the pictures before reading the written text should be stressed as an important study procedure.

170: Picture the Picture

Purpose: To provide practice in associating the text with the correct pictures.

Construction: Select a fiction book that has very descriptive passages. If possible, select a book that also contains numerous illustrations.

Players: Entire class

Materials: Fiction book, drawing paper, pencils

Directions: Read a descriptive passage aloud to the class from the selected fiction book. If possible, read a passage that corresponds to an illustration in the book. Direct the students to listen carefully for the descriptive adjectives that are contained in the passage. After the passage is read, have the students suggest what they believe the picture or scene described in the book would look like. A variation would be to have each student draw a picture to illustrate how he envisions each scene that was described. After the discussion and/or drawing, the illustration contained in the book should be shown to the students.

171: TV Plot Sequence

Purpose: To provide practice in following plot sequence.

Preparation: Instruct the students to watch a program on television that will have a follow-up episode or conclusion that can be viewed on a later day.

Players: Entire class

Materials: Pencils, paper

Directions: On the day after the students have seen the program, discuss with the class the various events that took place in the story. Establish the overall plot for the story and discuss some possible events that could happen in the next episode. At the conclusion of the class discussion, have the students break into groups of three or four children.

Appoint one of the members of each group as secretary or recorder. Direct the group to discuss what they believe will happen in the next episode of the program. Have the secretary of each group write a brief summary of their idea of the conclusion of the story. If more than one event will be taking place in the next episode, have the events listed in the sequence in which the students believe they will occur. Collect the papers and display them on the bulletin board so that all members of the class can read them. When the next episode is televised, have the students watch it. The next day discuss in class whether or not they agree with the conclusion of the story. Have the secretary of each group read to the class the summary they prepared. Have the class select the summary or summaries they believe were as good as or better than the television episode.

172: Create a Sequence

Purpose: To provide practice in following plot sequence.

Construction: Obtain from magazines or books pictures that show something about to happen (such as a grizzly bear charging a hunter, a plane spiraling toward the ground, a girl or boy opening a door to find a surprise party, a car accident, etc.). If possible, mount the pictures on posterboard or stiff paper

Players: Entire class

Materials: Paper, pencils, books, magazines, posterboard, glue stick

Directions: Show a descriptive picture to the group and discuss with the students what the picture depicts. Do not discuss what happened before or after the event pictured. After the students have thoroughly discussed the picture, direct them to write in story form what they believe happened before and after the event pictured. The students should be encouraged to be as thorough as possible in their descriptions. They should also be encouraged to show a sequence of events that led up to the event pictured and a sequence of events that happened immediately after the event pictured. After the stories are written, the students should be encouraged to share them with the class. The stories can also be collected and bound into a volume. The cover of the volume should contain the picture and a brief description of the activity. The volume can be housed in the room library.

173: Mysterious Sequence

Purpose: To provide practice in following plot sequence.

Construction: Read two or three short mystery stories to the class. Discuss the story plots and the sequence of events that lead to the solution of the mysteries. Sequence charts can be developed so that the class can see the events that led to the solution of the mystery.

Example:

SEQUENCE CHART
1. Man murdered
2. Body discovered by butler
3. Murder witness discovered
4. Witness disappears
5. Murder weapon discovered
        etc.

Players: Entire class

Materials: Book of short mystery stories, tape recorder, record player, records for background music, pencils, paper

Directions: After the class has listened to and discussed mystery stories, have the students create their own mystery story as a group. Write the class's story on newsprint paper. It should be written in play form and should include characters who have designated dialogue. After the story has been written, review and revise it with the class until you and the class are satisfied that it is a good mystery story with a good plot sequence. As you are guiding the class in the writing of the story be sure to emphasize the plot sequence. After the story has been revised, have the class select students to read each of the character parts. Select one student to operate a tape recorder and one or two students to select background music for the story. As the students read the story into the tape recorder, have the music played softly in the background. You should caution the readers and the other students who are helping with the recording that it may take several attempts before the tape is correctly done. When the tape is completed, the class may wish to invite another class to hear their mystery story.

174: Classification Strips

Purpose: To provide practice in classifying information under appropriate categories.

Construction: Cut several strips of oaktag that are long enough to have four words printed horizontally on them. On each strip, print three words that can be classified under one heading and one word that does not belong such as poodle, setter, collie, Siamese or Harrisburg, Atlanta, Richmond, Australia. For this activity, use words from subject areas that have been studied (geography, history, math, science, etc.) On the back of the strip print the one word that does not belong with the other three words. Laminate each strip or cover it with clear Con-Tact paper. Place the strips in a pile on a table.

Players: One or two

Materials: Oaktag, scissors, grease pencil, clear Con-Tact paper or laminating materials

Directions: If one student is playing, he selects a strip and underlines the word that does not belong with the other three words. He checks his answer by looking on the back of the strip. If two students are playing, they will alternate turns selecting a strip from the pile. The student gives his answer, and the other student will check the answer on the back of the strip. If the student's answer is correct, he will keep the strip. If the answer is incorrect, the strip is placed on the bottom of the pile. The winner is the student with the most strips.

175: Classification Folders

Purpose: To provide practice in classifying information under appropriate categories.

Construction: Use Manila file folders to create individual classification study folders. Print in large letters on the inside top half of the file folder the classification subject (Presidents, Shellfish, Inventors, Farm Equipment, etc.). Print this same classification on the tab of the file folder. Glue an envelope to the bottom half of the file folder. Cut strips out of oaktag, making them long enough to have one word printed on them. On the strips for each file folder, print several topic words that fit the classification subject and several words that do not fit. Words that do not fit the classification subject can be coded on the back by placing a dot in the upper right-hand corner of the strip. Place all of the strips in the envelope.

Players: One

Materials: Oaktag, file folders, envelopes, glue stick, scissors

Directions: The student will select a file folder and take the classification strips out of the envelope. All strips should be placed face up in a pile. The student will group the strips into two piles: words that fit the classification subject and words that do not. When all strips have been placed on one of the piles, the student checks the back of each strip to determine if it has been correctly classified. Students should be encouraged to ask the teacher about the strips that have been incorrectly classified.

176: Team Classification

Purpose: To provide practice in classifying information under appropriate categories.

Construction: On the chalkboard, print titles that can be used to classify selected topics (Explorers, Inventors, Warriors, Countries, Fruits, Presidents, Flowers, etc.). Print on 3″ × 5″ index cards words that fit into the listed classifications. Place the cards in a small box. All words printed on the cards should be from lessons or stories that were studied.

Players: Entire class or small group

Materials: Index cards (3″ × 5″), chalkboard, two colors of chalk, small box, marker

Directions: Divide the group into two teams that will alternate turns. Select one of the word cards from the box. The team member whose turn it is will read the word aloud and identify the category under which it belongs. If his answer is correct, he writes the word under the correct category on the chalkboard. Each team will use a different color chalk to write the words on the chalkboard. If an incorrect answer is given, the opposite team will have an opportunity to categorize the word. If their answer is correct, they may write the word on the chalkboard using their color chalk. They will then attempt to categorize the next word that you draw from the box. The game continues until all the cards have been drawn. Cards that are missed by both teams are returned to the box. Those words are retaught by you at a later time. The winner of the game is the team that has the most words written on the chalkboard in its color chalk.

177: Cause-and-Effect Matching

Purpose: To provide practice in determining cause-and-effect relationships

Construction: On strips of oaktag, print words or phrases that are either a cause or an effect, and punch a hole in the middle of the strip. Each cause statement strip must have a matching effect statement strip. Place all the cause strips in an envelope labeled "Causes" and all the effect statement strips in an envelope labeled "Effects." On a large piece of posterboard, attach Christmas tree ornament hooks in two vertical rows. Space them far enough apart so that the oaktag strips can hang freely on them. Label the row of hooks on the left "Cause" and the row of hooks on the right "Effect."

Example:

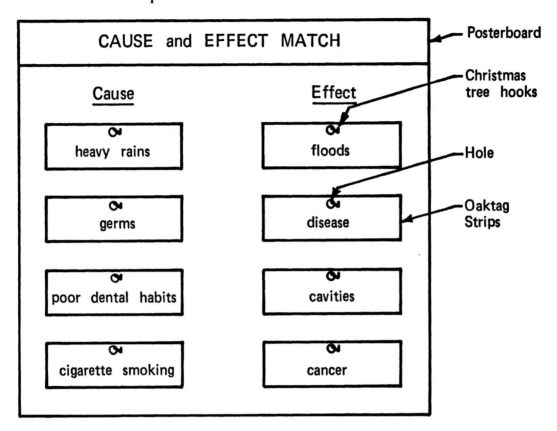

Players: One or two

Materials: Large piece of posterboard, Christmas tree ornament hooks, marker, two envelopes, oaktag strips, scissors, paper punch

Directions: The oaktag strips in the envelopes are placed on a table, the "causes" in one pile and the "effects" in another. The player selects a strip from the "cause" pile and attempts to find its matching effect in the other pile. If he is successful, the two strips are hung across from each other in the appropriate columns on the posterboard chart. If a match is not found or an incorrect effect is identified, the strips are returned to their piles on the table. When there is one player, he continues the activity until he has matched all the strips he can. When there are two players, they alternate turns and the winner is the player who matches the most causes and effects. The activity can be made self-correcting by placing numbers on the backs of the strips so that the matching cause-and-effect strips have the same number.

178: Cause-and-Effect Pictures

Purpose: To provide practice in determining cause-and-effect relationships.

Construction: Cut pictures out of magazines or draw them yourself. The pictures must illustrate actions or situations that have identifiable causes. Glue or draw the pictures on pieces of posterboard. On 3″ × 5″ index cards print a "cause" statement to match each picture. Place all the pictures in an envelope or folder labeled "Effect" and the index cards in an envelope labeled "Cause." Examples of possible pictures and their corresponding cause statements would be as follows:

PICTURES	CAUSE STATEMENT
1. Decorated Christmas tree	1. Christmas is tomorrow.
2. Smashed car fender	2. The car hit a pole.
3. Man putting chains on his car's tires	3. Snow was falling very fast.
4. Skydiver caught in a tree	4. The wind had shifted.
5. Mailman being bitten by a dog	5. The dog was left in the yard.
6. Football player catching a touchdown pass	6. The quarterback threw a long pass.
7. Boy picking a tomato off a tomato plant	7. The boy had planted a seed two months ago.

Players: One or two

Materials: Index cards (3″ × 5″), posterboard, pictures from magazines, scissors, glue, marker, envelopes, folder

Directions: The index cards and the pictures are placed face up on a table, the index cards in one pile and the pictures in another. The player selects an index card from the pile and attempts to match it with the appropriate picture in the picture pile. If he is successful, the index card is placed on top of the picture and both are placed on the table in front of the player. If his match is incorrect, the picture and the card are returned to the bottom of their piles. When there is one player, he continues the activity until he has matched as many cards and pictures as he can. When there are two players, they alternate turns and the winner is the player who has the most matches placed on the table in front of him. The activity can be made self-correcting by placing numbers on the backs of the index cards and the pictures so that the matching cause-and-effect have the same number.

179: Cause-and-Effect Composition

Purpose: To provide practice in determining cause-and-effect relationships.

Construction: Collect pictures to develop a picture file. The pictures must illustrate actions or situations that have identifiable causes such as a person with a broken leg, a broken window, a car with a flat tire, a race driver holding a trophy, etc. Mount the pictures on posterboard and place them in a file box or folder.

Players: Entire class or individuals

Materials: Writing paper, pencils, file box or folder, pictures

Directions: Each student selects a picture from the file. He examines the picture and writes a short paragraph about what caused the result pictured. After the students have completed their written explanations, they can share their paragraphs with the class. The picture and the written paragraph can be displayed on the bulletin board.

180: Summary One-Liners

Purpose: To provide practice in summarizing material.

Construction: Cut out of magazines or newspapers descriptive pictures or news articles. Mount the pictures or articles on oaktag and cover them with clear Con-Tact paper or laminate them. Place them in a large brown paper envelope and label the envelope "Summary One-Liners."

Players: One or entire class

Materials: Large brown envelope, magazines, newspapers, scissors, oaktag, clear Con-Tact paper or laminating materials, glue, grease pencil

Directions: Students will select one or more pictures and articles. The students are instructed to write a one-sentence caption on the bottom of the picture or at the top of the news article. An answer key of possible captions can be attached to the back of the picture or article. Students who are doing the exercise with a group can discuss their choice of caption with the group.

181: Summarization Cards

Purpose: To provide practice in summarizing material.

Construction: Print three or more descriptive phrases about a particular event, place, or person on a piece of posterboard. Leave a blank space at the top of the posterboard so that the student may write a summary phrase. Cover the posterboard with clear Con-Tact paper or laminate it. Make several different cards and store them in an envelope.

Cards can be made about material studied in history, geography, science, or other subject areas. Number the cards in the upper right-hand corner. Prepare an answer key listing each card by number and giving a correct summary phrase.

Example:

Summary _____¹ 1. Sinking of Battleship Arizona 2. Japanese surprise attack on Pearl Harbor 3. Many American soldiers killed 4. Attack thought to be a false alarm	Summary _____² 1. Rats infest cities 2. Many people ill 3. Fleas found to carry disease

Answer Key

    Card 1: America Enters World War II

    Card 2: Cause of Bubonic Plague Is Fleas

Players: One or small group

Materials: Posterboard, clear Con-Tact paper or laminating materials, grease pencil, scissors, envelope

Directions: The students will select a descriptive card, read the phrases listed on it, and print a summary phrase at the top that identifies the event, place, or person being described. The student may check his answer on the answer key.

182: Comic Strip Summary

Purpose: To provide practice in summarizing material.

Construction: Cut several comic strips out of the newspaper. Do not cut them into separate frames. Place the comic strips in envelopes—one comic strip per envelope. On the back of each envelope print three phrases, one of which best summarizes the action shown in the comic strip in that envelope. Number each envelope in the top right-hand corner. Place the envelopes in a shoe box and place the box on a table in the classroom. Make an answer key that shows the correct summarization statement for each comic strip. Keep the answer key at your desk. Paste the directions for doing the exercise to the top of the shoe box lid.

Players: One or small group

Materials: Comic sections of newspapers, scissors, envelopes, paper, marker, shoe box

Directions: The student follows the directions pasted on the shoe box lid.

Example:

DIRECTIONS:

1. Select an envelope.
2. Take the comic strip out of the envelope.
3. Study the comic strip.
4. Turn to the back of the envelope and identify the phrase that summarizes what is happening in the comic strip.
5. Find the number in the top right-hand corner of the envelope and write it on your paper. Beside this number, copy the answer from the back of the envelope that you think best summarizes the comic strip.
6. Repeat this procedure for all the envelopes.
7. After you have completed all of the comic strips, check your answers with the key on the teacher's desk.

ACTIVITIES THAT IMPROVE CRITICAL READING SKILLS

The following activities teach the pupil to identify and understand figures of speech and to detect and interpret propaganda techniques.

183: Simile and Metaphor List

Purpose: To provide practice in identifying and understanding figures of speech.

Construction: Print the definitions for simile and metaphor on the chalkboard. Underneath each definition write four or five examples of each figure of speech.

Players: Entire class or small group

Materials: Chalkboard, chalk, paper, pencils

Directions: Explain the definitions of simile and metaphor to the students. Stress that similes and metaphors add interest to compositions by conveying a clear and sharp image of the object being described (hungry as a bear, big as a house, an icy stare). After the students understand the two figures of speech, ask them to create similes and metaphors about objects in the room or about objects that are familiar to them. Students are to write their examples on a sheet of paper.

Examples:

Simile

1. Our house is like an overstuffed suitcase.
2. Her dress has as many colors as a rainbow.
3. The room is as warm as toast.

Metaphor

1. The scent of the flowers was a beautiful perfume.
2. The sun was a river of light.
3. He had the quickness of a cat.

When the students have had sufficient time, ask them to read their similes and metaphors aloud and share them with the class. As a conclusion to the exercise, ask the students to bring to the next class session an example of a poem or story that contains similes and metaphors.

134

184: Figure of Speech Composition

Purpose: To provide practice in identifying and understanding figures of speech.

Construction: On the chalkboard write a story or poem that contains examples of personification, simile, and metaphor. Underline all of the examples of personification, simile, and metaphor contained in the writing. Color code the underlining by using a different color chalk for each figure of speech.

Players: Entire class or small group

Materials: Short story or poem, chalkboard, chalk in several colors

Directions: Discuss the story or poem with the class, emphasizing the meaning and use of the three figures of speech. Give the students additional examples of personification, simile, and metaphor. When the students understand the figures of speech, have the class develop on the chalkboard a composition that includes examples of personification, simile, and metaphor. Use the different colors of chalk as before to underline the three figures of speech. A follow-up assignment would be for the students to bring to class examples of personification, simile, and metaphor that they have found in newspapers and magazines.

185: Figurative Search

Purpose: To provide practice in identifying and understanding figures of speech.

Construction: Provide the students with a variety of books, magazines, and newspapers. These resources will be used to locate examples of personification, simile, metaphor, idioms, and euphemism.

Players: Entire class

Materials: Writing paper, pens, magazines, books, newspapers

Directions: Divide the class into groups with two or three students on each team. On the chalkboard write the definitions of the figures of speech and give examples of each one.

Example:

PERSONIFICATION—gives human qualities to an object that is not human
The big fish was king of the sea.
The wind walks on the grass.

SIMILE—comparison of two unlike things and uses the words <u>like</u>, <u>as</u>, or <u>than</u>

The dewdrops at dawn were like pearls of light.
The clipper ships were as stately as churches.

METAPHOR—compares two unlike objects but does not use the words <u>like</u>, <u>as</u>, or <u>than</u>

The moon is a spotlight shining in the sky.
The automobiles were phantoms in the fog.

IDIOM—short, local expression

in a nutshell, on the other hand, caught his eye

EUPHEMISM—substitution of an agreeable expression for an offensive one

plump for fat, slender for skinny

Discuss the definitions with the class. When the students understand the examples and the concepts of the five figures of speech, have them work as teams to locate and list examples of each figure of speech. Instruct the students to copy the example and note where it was found. They should identify the figure of speech each example illustrates and also explain what the expression means in ordinary language. The team is awarded one point for each correct example, identification, and interpretation. Each team must have examples for each of the five figures of speech. Assign a time limit for the activity. The winner is the team that has the most points.

186: Critical Reader

Purpose: To provide practice in detecting and interpreting propaganda techniques.

Construction: List and define the following propaganda techniques on strips of oaktag and attach them to a bulletin board:

1. TESTIMONIALS—having a popular or respected person endorse a product.
2. GLITTERING GENERALITIES—using vague phrases or statements to influence a person's point of view.
3. BANDWAGON—making believe that everyone else is doing something or using something so you should also.
4. EMOTIONALLY CHARGED WORDS—using negative words to create an unfavorble reaction to a person or product.
5. PLAIN FOLK TALK—acting, dressing, or talking like the common people to influence the people.
6. CARD STACKING—telling only one side of an issue and omitting the other side.
7. TRANSFER TECHNIQUE—associating a respected symbol or organization with a particular product.

To the right of each definition, place a pocket or folder.

Players: Entire class

Materials: Oaktag, marker, scissors, construction paper or folders to make the pockets

Directions: Discuss with the class how a critical reader questions what he reads, analyzes the content, and reacts to the material. Explain to the students how propaganda techniques are used as a method of influencing consumers. Discuss in detail each of the seven propaganda techniques listed on the bulletin board. Give examples of each technique from local newspapers, magazines, etc. When the students understand the concept, ask them to bring to class as many examples of each propaganda technique as they can find. Copy each example or glue it to a strip of oaktag. Place the examples on the bulletin board in the pockets beside the appropriate techniques. After the students have had the opportunity to read the examples and become familiar with them, take the examples out of the pockets and discuss them with the class. See if the students agree with the classification of each example. Have the class react to the propaganda technique and see if they agree with the claim it makes for the product represented.

187: Silly Products

Purpose: To provide practice in detecting and interpreting propaganda techniques.

Construction: Type names of "silly" products such as Gloopy Gum, Super Shine Car Wax, Perfect Pizza, Lassie's Frozen Doggie Dinners, etc. on a ditto master. Leave space after each product name so that an advertising slogan can be written by the student.

Players: Entire class

Materials: Typewriter, ditto master, pencils

Directions: After you have discussed propaganda techniques (see activity 186) with your class, have them complete the ditto sheet by creating a slogan or claim for a "silly" product name that they believe would influence a consumer to purchase the product. After the slogan or claim, have the student identify the propaganda technique that he has used. Collect the papers and correct the students' work. Slogans that are especially imaginative should be shared with the class. The class should be asked to identify the propaganda technique utilized in each example read. A variation of the activity would be to have the students use the best examples as the basis for mock television commercials.

188: Name That Product

Purpose: To provide practice in detecting and interpreting propaganda techniques.

Construction: On 5″ × 8″ index cards, print various slogans, phrases, jingles, etc. that are used as propaganda techniques in advertising popular products that the students will be able to identify. Print on the back of each card the propaganda technique (see activity 186) that is being used and the name of the product it is describing. Place the cards face up in a pile on a table.

Players: Two

Materials: Index cards (5″ × 8″), marker

Directions: The players alternate drawing a card from the pile. After the card is drawn, the player must identify the propaganda technique being used. If he can identify the technique, he keeps the card and receives one point. If he can also tell what product is being described, he will receive an additional two points. If a player does not correctly identify the propaganda technique, the card is placed on the bottom of the pile. The winner is the player who has the most points.

Section 6

ACTIVITIES TO IMPROVE ORAL READING SKILLS

ORAL READING ACTIVITIES

Activities included in this section are designed to provide practice in pronouncing words correctly, using appropriate voice intonation, pitch, and stress, and using punctuation marks correctly when reading aloud. Additional activities also help the pupil to read aloud with correct phrasing, with clear and distinct enunciation and appropriate expression, and with appropriate eye-voice span.

189: Bank-a-Word

Players: To provide practice in pronouncing words correctly.

Construction: Each student will need a file box labeled with his name. The file box may be metal or cardboard, but it must be large enough to hold 3″ × 5″ index cards. Each student will also need a supply of blank 3″ × 5″ index cards.

Players: Entire class

Materials: Metal or cardboard file boxes, index cards (3″ × 5″), pencils, rubber stamp

Directions: Each time the student encounters a word that he does not know how to pronounce, he prints it on an index card. The words may be new sight words or vocabulary words that are read in any subject area (science, geography, history, etc.). After printing the word on the index card, the student will look up the word in a dictionary and print the phonetic spelling of the word on the back of the card. The student will practice pronouncing the word until he knows it. When he has accumulated five new words that he can correctly pronounce without referring to the phonetic spelling, he will take the word cards up to the teacher for deposit. To enter them in his account (file box), he must pronounce them correctly for the teacher. Each word that is correctly pronounced is stamped with a validation stamp (rubber stamp with animal, clown, etc.). These cards are then placed in the file box in alphabetical order.

To keep a record of how many words each student is learning, the teacher keeps a record sheet for each child. When the words are entered in the student's account (file box), the teacher writes the words on the child's record sheet and places the date beside them. The record sheet will help the teacher see how many words the student is learning. The words on the sheet can also be used for planning individual activities for each child.

A variation of the exercise would be to give the child special privileges after he "banks" a specified number of words. The privileges can be special activities such as going to the library or having a free reading period.

140

190: Round 10

Purpose: To provide practice in pronouncing words correctly.

Construction: On a ditto master, type a gamesheet that has five vertical columns labeled "Person," "Place," "Color," "Object," and "SCORE." Print one letter of the alphabet on each of 26 index cards (3″ × 5″ size). Place these alphabet cards in a pile face down on the table.

Players: Two or small group

Materials: Ditto master, index cards (3″ × 5″)

Directions: Distribute a dittoed gamesheet to each player. One player is chosen by the group to select the alphabet cards from the pile. To play the game, a card is selected from the alphabet pile and shown to all of the players. Each player will attempt to write one word that begins with the same sound as the letter drawn under each of the four categories (Person, Place, Color, Object). When the students have written the words on their gamesheets, they will take turns reading their answers aloud. To determine each player's score, use the following criteria:

1. Score zero points if an incorrect answer is given in any category or if the player pronounces the word incorrectly.
2. Score one point for each category that has a correct answer that is pronounced correctly.
3. Each player records his total number correct for that letter in the "SCORE" column.

The winner of the game is the player who has the highest total score after ten letters have been completed. The exercise can be continued for as many rounds of ten words as you wish. If more than one round is played, the winner is the player who has the highest total score.

191: Pronunciation Match

Purpose: To provide practice in pronouncing words correctly.

Construction: Obtain four boxes large enough to hold several 3″ × 5″ index cards. On 3″ × 5″ index cards print four sounds that are to be practiced (for example, oi, ü, ĭ, and ă). On additional 3″ × 5″ index cards print words that contain the four sounds that are to be practiced. To make the boxes for the activity, tape one of the cards with a sound printed on it to the front of each box and attach an answer key to the bottom of the box showing which words contain that sound. Place the word cards in a pile and the boxes beside them.

Players: One

Materials: Four small boxes, index cards (3″ × 5″), marker, tape

Directions: The child selects a word card from the pile. He pronounces the word aloud and places it in the box he believes matches the sound in the word. When he has completed all the word cards, he checks the word cards he has placed in each box with the answer keys on the bottoms of the boxes. Words that are missed are shown to you for further review.

192: Explanation-Response

Purpose: To provide practice in using appropriate voice intonation, pitch, and stress in reading aloud.

Construction: On several 5″ × 8″ index cards, print sentences that express dialogue relating to an incident in sports or other situations. The sentences should be able to be read in different ways depending upon the mood the reader wishes to reflect (fear, joy, sadness, disbelief, anger, surprise, etc.). Each card should contain at least two sentences; however, if you wish to provide more practice, additional responses can be written. Place the cards in an envelope or small box.

Examples:

Card 1 (representing a call by a football referee and a player's response. The underlined word(s) should be emphasized.)

Referee: You are offside, Number 68.

Response 1   Player: I was offside?

Response 2   Player: I was offside?

Response 3   Player: I was offside.

Card 2 (representing a call by a tennis line judge and a player's response. The underlined word(s) should be emphasized.)

Tennis line judge: The ball was out.

Response 1   Player: The ball was out.

Response 2   Player: The ball was out?

Players: Entire class or small group

Materials: Index cards (5″ × 8″), marker or pen, envelope or small box

Directions: The players take turns selecting one of the cards from the envelope or box and reading the sentences printed on the card. Each sentence must be read according to where the inflection, pitch, or stress is intended. The other players must then guess what mood is reflected by each sentence as it is read aloud to the group

Example:

Card 1

Referee: You are offside, Number 68.

Response 1   Player: I was offside? (mood reflected is disbelief)

Response 2   Player: I was offside? (mood reflected is anger)

Response 3   Player: I was offside. (mood reflected is sad agreement)

The exercise is used as a reinforcement exercise for teaching intonation, stress, and pitch. If the exercise is to be done without your supervision, the mood for each sentence can be written on the back of the card.

193: Product Advertising

Purpose: To provide practice in using appropriate voice intonation, pitch, and stress in reading aloud.

Construction: Students create names for household products (Pearly Toothpaste, Spring Fresh Soap, etc.) and print them on pieces of paper. Attach the papers to various empty containers to represent the products.

Players: Entire class or small group

Materials: Paper, markers or pens, various empty containers

Directions: Each student selects one of the products, creates a slogan for it, and prepares a commercial message about it. To convey the desired meaning, you will need to discuss with each student which words in the message he has written will need special emphasis when read aloud. After the student writes the message and has it reviewed by you, he reads it aloud to the group.

A variation of the exercise is to have small groups create the commercial message rather than having each individual student writing a message. You will find that the group messages may be more creative than the individual ones. By having groups write the messages and one member of the group read his group's message to the class, you will also reduce the amount of time that is necessary for the reading.

194: Play Practice

Purpose: To use appropriate voice intonation, pitch, and stress to give meaning to material read aloud.

Construction: A play will be written by the class or commercial copies of a short play will be distributed to each member of the group.

Players: Entire class or small group

Materials: Copies of the play written by the class or commercial play books

Directions: Give each student in the group a copy of the play written by the class or the commercial play books. Have the group select students to read each character part. The students will practice their parts so that they can use the appropriate voice intonation, pitch, and stress. When they are ready, they will read the play for the group to enjoy.

195: Punctuation Signs

Purpose: To provide practice in recognizing and responding to simple punctuation marks.

Construction: A paragraph is printed on a large piece of posterboard or on the chalkboard. Using colored pencils or chalk, color each period red and each comma yellow.

Players: Small group

Materials: Posterboard or chalkboard, marker and colored pencils or chalk

Directions: Discuss with the group the significance of the colors used for the punctuation marks (red-stop-period; yellow-slow-comma). Compare the colors to the traffic signals of the same color. An analogy should be drawn between the traffic lights and the colors. When the students understand how the colors are to be used as they read aloud, have them take turns reading sentences from the posterboard or chalkboard. A student who "runs over" a punctuation mark may be issued a traffic ticket for speeding.

196: Punctuation Tic Tac Toe

Purpose: To provide practice in recognizing and interpreting end punctuation marks.

Construction: Using masking tape, make a large tic tac toe board on the floor. Cut several large squares out of posterboard. The squares should be large enough to hold three sentences and small enough to fit inside the tic tac toe squares. On each posterboard square, print the same sentence three times, each time ending the sentence with a different punctuation mark as the following example illustrates:

> That's your car.
> That's your car?
> That's your car!

Using ten additional posterboard squares, make five "X" cards and five "0" cards. Give the "X" cards to one player and the "0" cards to the other.

Players: Two

Materials: Beanbag, masking tape, posterboard, marker

Directions: Tape a posterboard square in each of the nine squares on the tic tac toe board. Mark the toss line with a piece of masking tape. Each student will stand on this line and toss the beanbag onto the tic tac toe board. If he misses on the first try, he may toss again before he loses his turn. After the player tosses the beanbag, he reads aloud each of the sentences contained in the square. He must use appropriate voice inflection to convey the meaning of the end punctuation mark. If he reads the sentences correctly, he removes the card and places his "X" or "O" card in its place. The first player to place three of his "X" or "O" cards in a line (horizontally, diagonally, or vertically) wins the game. The rules of tic tac toe apply.

197: Picture Punctuation

Purpose: To provide practice in recognizing how commas affect meaning.

Construction: Cut a sheet of construction paper into two pieces. Paste a picture to the top half and print a descriptive sentence on the bottom half before cutting.

Examples:

Top half—A picture of two men washing a car
Bottom half—Bobby Joe, and Steve are washing the car.

Top half—A picture of three men washing a car
Bottom half—Bobby Joe, and Steve are washing the car.

Several pairs such as the examples given above should be made. Place the pictures on one section of a table and the sentences on another section.

Players: One or two

Materials: Pictures, construction paper, paste, scissors, marker

Directions: Each player selects a picture and matches it with the correct sentence. The activity can be made self-correcting by placing corresponding numbers on the backs of cards that are correct matches. If two players complete the activity, the winner is the player who correctly matches the most pictures and sentences.

198: Story Phrasing

Purpose: To provide practice in reading with correct phrasing.

Construction: Type a few short stories on a ditto master. The stories should be marked so that the phrasing is indicated.

Example:

> As Mike/ walked through the woods/ he spotted/ a fallen deer./ The young deer/ had injured its leg./ As Mike/ approached the animal,/ it began/ to thrash and squirm./ To stop the animal/ from thrashing and squirming/ and perhaps further injuring itself,/ Mike carefully marked the spot/ where the deer lay/ and he ran back/ to get his father,/ the veterinarian./ He and his father returned,/ tranquilized the deer,/ and transported it/ to their house./ Mike's father/ treated the animal's broken leg/ and nursed it/ back to health.

Players: Entire class or small group

Materials: Ditto masters, paper, pencils

Directions: Give each student in the group a copy of the story. Discuss with them why the story is divided into phrases. Read the story aloud and observe the phrasing that is indicated. Have the students read the story aloud in unison with you.

As a follow-up activity, distribute another ditto sheet with an unmarked story typed on it. Have the students mark the phrasing in the story. This follow-up activity should only be done when you believe your students understand the concept of phrasing.

199: Phrase Flasher

Purpose: To provide practice in reading with correct phrasing.

Construction: Make flashcards out of strips of oaktag and print phrases on them. The cards should be large enough so that all students in the group can see them.

Players: Small group

Materials: Oaktag strips, marker, scissors

Directions: Flash the cards to the students in the group and have them volunteer to tell what was printed on the card. Be sure to hold the cards in a position where they can be seen by all the students in the group.

A variation of the exercise is to print phrases from a story on a series of cards. Flash the cards in sequence and have the group read them aloud in unison.

200: Phrase Detective

Purpose: To provide practice with phrasing and interpreting meaning.

Construction: Type the words "WHO," "WHAT," "WHERE," and "WHEN" on a ditto master, leaving room under each word so that phrases can be written. Distribute a copy of the ditto to each student in the group. Print several phrases from a story on the chalkboard. The phrases must be written so that they can be placed under one of the four categories on the ditto: WHO, WHAT, WHERE, or WHEN.

Players: Small group

Materials: Ditto master, paper, pencils

Directions: Instruct the students to read the phrases silently and write each phrase under the appropriate word on their ditto sheets. When all the students have completed the exercise, read the phrases aloud and identify the word they should be listed under. Any questions that arise about the placement of the phrases should be discussed with the group.

Examples:

Who	What
General George Patton	World War II
Astronaut John Glenn	American Space Program

Where	When
Europe and Germany	The year 1943
Cape Canaveral, Florida	During the 1960s

201: Story Expression

Purpose: To provide practice in reading aloud with clear and distinct enunciation and appropriate expression.

Construction: Write or obtain a story that can be tape recorded in your classroom. Divide the story into sections of three or four paragraphs each, and select one student to read each section aloud. Each student should receive a copy of the story with his specific part marked.

Players: Entire class or small group

Materials: Tape recorder, copies of a story

Directions: The story will be read aloud by the students (each student reading his assigned three- or four-paragraph section) so that it can be recorded on the tape recorder. After the story has been recorded, the tape is played back to the group. The students will listen and decide whether or not they have read the story correctly and with the appropriate expression. If time permits, the story may be recorded a second time giving the students an opportunity to improve their oral reading based on the group's critique of the first reading.

202: Expression Dog

Purpose: To provide practice in reading aloud with clear and distinct enunciation and appropriate expression.

Construction: Make a dachshund out of construction paper. Attach the head to one side of a bulletin board and the tail section to the other side. Using construction paper, cut out several sections for the middle part of the dachshund. These sections will be placed on a table near the bulletin board and attached one piece at a time.

Example:

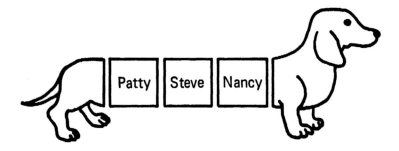

Players: Entire class

Materials: Construction paper, marker, scissors, staples, staple gun

Directions: During each reading period, have some members of the class read aloud from their readers or from other books. If a student reads the material with appropriate enunciation and expression, he writes his name on a middle section of the dachshund and attaches it to the bulletin board. Each student must have an opportunity to place his name on the dog. When the dog is completed, another one can be started.

203: Expression Collection

Purpose: To provide practice in reading aloud with clear and distinct enunciation and appropriate expression.

Construction: Assemble a collection of famous quotations, sayings, riddles, poems, song refrains, etc., and print them on 3″ × 5″ index cards. Included in the collection should be material for holidays, special occasions, months of the year, etc. To make the collection more accessible, it should be divided into categories.

Players: Entire class

Materials: Index cards (3″ × 5″), file box, pen

Directions: Set aside a certain time of the day or week for this activity. During this special time, the students will take turns reading aloud one selection from the collection. To insure that the student will be prepared to read the selection to the class, he should be allowed to take the index card home the day before to rehearse.

The activity could be used as the "Thought for the Day." If an intercom system is used for announcements in the school, the students could take turns reading the "Thought for the Day" over the school intercom.

204: Pacing

Purpose: To provide practice in reading with an appropriate eye-voice span.

Construction: Give each student a reader (or other book to read from) and a 3″ × 5″ index card.

Players: One or entire class

Materials: Index cards (3″ × 5″), reading materials

Directions: Students take turns reading aloud to the class or individually to the teacher. The student will pace his reading by using an index card to cover the words that have been read. The student will move the index card along the text as he reads.

205: Flash-a-Phrase

Purpose: To provide practice in reading with an appropriate eye-voice span.

Construction: Make a tachistoscope and flash strips out of oaktag. To make the tachistoscope, cut two pieces of oaktag so that they are the same length and width. In one piece of oaktag cut a window that will be wide enough to expose two- and three-word phrases. Staple the outer edges of the tachistoscope. Cut a strip of oaktag long enough to fit through the tachistoscope and wide enough to write two- and three-word phrases on it. This strip will be the flash strip.

Example:

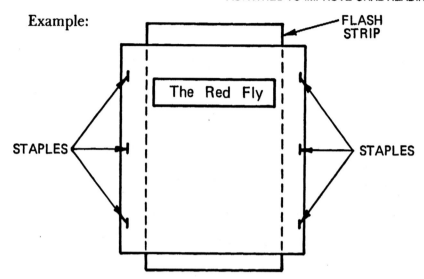

Players: Two for each tachistoscope

Materials: Oaktag, scissors, staples, stapler, marker or pen

Directions: One of the two students will flash the phrases and the other student will be the reader. The phrases should be exposed for one-half second. It will be necessary for you to show the students how to use the tachistoscope. The purpose of the activity should be carefully explained to the students so that they will not attempt to trick each other with the flashed phrase. Each student must realize that his purpose is to help his partner increase his eye-voice span.

A variation of the activity is to print the phrases on oaktag strips and flash the strips to the student.

206: Controlled Reading

Purpose: To provide practice in reading with the appropriate eye-voice span

Construction: Obtain a controlled reader and appropriate film strips.

Players: Small group

Materials: Controlled reader, film strips

Directions: Use the controlled reader to pace the students as they read aloud. Set the controlled reader on an appropriate speed. Use the shadow setting and have each student practice reading aloud. Set the speed to accommodate each student's needs. Stress to the group that to be successful oral readers they must look ahead of the words they are pronouncing. Be certain that your speed setting does not establish a rate that is too fast for the reader.

Section 7

ACTIVITIES TO IMPROVE SURVIVAL READING SKILLS

ACTIVITIES FOR INTERPRETING AND COMPLETING FORMS

The following two activities are designed to help your students gain skill in understanding how to interpret and complete forms. Based on these exercises, you may wish to develop a file of your own activities to give your students experience in completing a variety of forms. Try to locate forms that will have particular significance for them. Students may also bring to class forms that they have had to complete.

207: Magazine Subscription

Purpose: To provide practice in interpreting information contained in a magazine subscription.

Introduction: If you plan to read a particular magazine on a regular basis, you may want to save money by subscribing to that magazine. Read the subscription information below and on a separate sheet of paper answer the questions that follow.

Form:

CRAFTS MAGAZINE SUBSCRIPTION INFORMATION

You can receive twelve issues of CRAFTS magazine, a magazine for children 8 to 12 years old. To receive your one-year subscription, mail in the postage-paid card. No money needs to be sent with the card. You will be billed at a later time. The current issue of CRAFTS will be sent to you and you will be billed at the special introductory rate of $12.00 (including postage and handling). This offer is $4.00 less than the cover price and $2.00 less than the regular subscription rate.

If you are not thoroughly delighted with your first issue, mark "cancelled" on your billing statement and return it to CRAFTS magazine. Your subscription will be voided and you will owe no money. You can keep the first issue as a gift. If you decide to cancel your subscription at a later time, you will receive a full refund for any issues not mailed.

I want CRAFTS sent to _____ (name of child) _____

☐ Enter one-year subscription—12 issues—and bill me $12.00 including postage and handling.

☐ Enter two-year subscription—24 issues—and bill me $22.00 including postage and handling.

Billing Name _____

Billing Address _____
City _____
State _____ Zip _____

Please allow 6 to 8 weeks for the first issue to arrive.

FOR NEW SUBSCRIBERS ONLY.

Questions:

1. When compared to the price of buying CRAFTS at a newsstand, will you be saving money by subscribing to the magazine for one year? If so, how much?

2. For what age reader is the magazine written?

3. Are you required to send money with the subscription card?

4. If you are currently a subscriber to CRAFTS magazine, can you use this form to renew your subscription? How much more than this subscription rate is your regular renewal cost?

5. If you receive two issues of CRAFTS magazine and then decide to cancel your subscription, how much money will be refunded to you?

6. When can you expect to receive your first issue of CRAFTS?

7. If you think you will be reading the magazine on a regular basis, how much money would you save on the regular subscription rate by ordering two years rather than just one year?

8. Whose name do you write in the blank labeled "Billing Name"?

9. If you have never read CRAFTS magazine, how can you decide whether or not you would enjoy reading it?

Answer Key:

1. Yes. $4.00
2. Ages 8 through 12
3. No
4. No. $2.00

5. $10.00

6. In 6 to 8 weeks

7. $6.00

8. Parents or person who will pay for the subscription

9. Talk to some of your friends about the magazine, review an issue in your library, send for a sample issue, etc.

208: Record Club Subscription

Purpose: To provide practice in interpreting information contained in a record club subscription.

Introduction: If you enjoy listening to music, you may want to join a record club. Read the subscription information below and on a separate sheet of paper answer the questions that follow.

Cheap Record and Tape Company
P.O. Box 721
Chicago, Illinois 42314

   I am enclosing $1.89 (which includes 3¢ for my 10 selections plus $1.86 for shipping and handling). Please accept my membership application. I agree to buy ten additional records or tapes of my choice at regular club prices during the coming two years, and I may cancel my membership anytime after doing so.

Write in the names of the 10 selections you want for 3¢.

_____

_____

_____

Send my selections in the following type of recording:

____ 8-Track Cartridges   ____ Tape Cassettes

____ Reel Tapes   ____ Records

My main musical interest is (Check one):

____ Country   ____ Jazz (No cassettes)

____ Easy Listening   ____ Rock and Roll

Name (please print) _____

Address _____ Apt. No. _____

City _____ State _____ ZIP _____

This offer not available in Puerto Rico, Alaska, or Hawaii. Allow 4 weeks for records to arrive.

Questions:

1. What is the initial cost of joining the Cheap Record and Tape Club?
2. How many records or tapes must you buy in the next two years?
3. How much will you pay for each of the additional records or tapes that you agree to buy?
4. Will the records or tapes you purchase in the next two years be sold to you at a discount rate?
5. If, after buying five records or tapes from the club, you find that you can buy them at a local record shop for less than the club prices, can you cancel your club membership? When can you cancel?
6. Which type of music is not available on cassette tapes?
7. How many types of music (Country, Easy Listening, Jazz, Rock and Roll) are you asked to select?
8. If you live in an apartment, what specific information must you include when you fill in the blank for address?
9. List the localities in which this offer is not valid.
10. What type of writing must you use to complete this subscription form?

Answer Key:

1. $1.89
2. At least ten
3. Regular club prices; no exact price is indicated
4. Not stated
5. No. After buying ten records/tapes
6. Jazz
7. One
8. Apartment number
9. Puerto Rico, Alaska, Hawaii
10. Must be printing for name and address section

ACTIVITIES FOR INTERPRETING PRODUCT INFORMATION

The following seven activities are designed to help your students in interpreting information found on product labels. Specific examples included are toothpaste, batteries, first aid spray, cereal, fruit drink, bleach, and disinfectant.

To prepare these activities for use in the classroom, cut out the product label and paste it to a piece of posterboard. Below the product information, attach a list of questions typed on a sheet of paper. To make the exercise self-correcting, type the answer key on another sheet of paper and attach it to the back of the posterboard. To preserve the activity, cover the posterboard with clear Con-Tact paper or laminate it. The cards may be stored in folders or in envelopes.

209: Toothpaste

Purpose: To provide practice in interpreting information found on a product label.

Introduction: Good dental hygiene begins with regular brushing and regular dental check-ups. Read about the following toothpaste and see what claims the manufacturer makes for this product.

Product Information: A CREST toothpaste label reads as follows:

"CREST has been shown to be an effective decay-preventive dentifrice that can be of significant value when used in a conscientiously applied program of oral hygiene and regular professional care."

Council on Dental Therapeutics—American Dental Association

Made in U.S.A. by PROCTER & GAMBLE, Cincinnati, Ohio 45202

FLUORISTAT is a trademark for a proven decay-preventive composition (active ingredient: sodium fluoride).

The Proctor & Gamble Company. Used with permission.

Questions:

1. What does the word <u>dentifrice</u> mean?
2. What is the meaning of the phrase "an effective decay-preventive dentifrice"?
3. What is the meaning of "a conscientiously applied program of oral hygiene and regular professional care"?

4. Where would you telephone if you wanted to speak with a representative of the company that manufactures CREST?

5. How do you know that FLUORISTAT is a combination of ingredients and not just a single ingredient?

6. What is the active ingredient in FLUORISTAT?

7. Does the company guarantee that CREST will prevent tooth decay?

Answer Key:

1. Paste, powder, or liquid for cleaning the teeth

2. A toothpaste that helps prevent cavities when used as directed

3. Regular brushing and care of teeth at home and seeing a dentist for regular check-ups

4. Cincinnati, Ohio

5. FLUORISTAT is a trademark for a "composition" of ingredients.

6. Sodium fluoride

7. No

210: Batteries

Purpose: To provide practice in interpreting information found on a product label.

Introduction: Batteries come in various sizes and shapes and are used to power many devices. The following information describes one size battery. Read the descriptive information to learn more about it and its use.

Product Information: "EVEREADY" ALKALINE POWER CELLS

Union Carbide Corporation. Used with permission.

Questions:

1. What is the company's guarantee if a device is damaged by this battery?
2. Under what condition is the guarantee void (not in effect)?
3. When used in a toy, how much longer will the alkaline battery last than the flashlight battery?
4. What size batteries are these?
5. What battery is replaced by this battery?
6. What might happen if this battery is recharged or thrown into a fire?
7. Why does this package have test holes?
8. If you have trouble with a battery from this package, where would you write?
9. What is the brand name of these batteries?
10. These batteries can be used to power what four items?

Answer Key:

1. The company will repair or replace, at their option, any device damaged by this battery.
2. If the battery has been recharged
3. 150% longer
4. Size AAA
5. NEDA 24A 1.5 volt batteries
6. Battery may explode or leak
7. So you can test whether or not the batteries are working when you purchase them
8. Union Carbide Corporation, P.O. Box 6056, Cleveland, Ohio 44101
9. Eveready
10. Flashlight, toy, radio, calculator

211: First Aid Spray

Purpose: To provide practice in interpreting information found on a product label.

Introduction: Medicine can be very helpful. However, when it is not used according to directions, it can also be harmful. Read the product information below to learn how to use this first aid spray correctly.

Product Information: BACTINE brand Skin Wound Cleanser

INDICATIONS: FIRST AID SPRAY TO CLEAN SUPER-FICIAL SKIN WOUNDS

Contains a safe and effective nonirritating antimicrobial (germ killing) ingredient. Does not delay wound healing.

DIRECTIONS: To spray, hold bottle upright 2 to 3 inches from wound and squeeze repeatedly to direct spray across wound. To flush, invert bottle and squeeze firmly to direct stream across wound. Apply to affected area until excess drains freely and wound is thoroughly clean. To aid in removing foreign particles, dab wound with clean gauze saturated with product.

WARNINGS: FOR EXTERNAL USE ONLY. Avoid spraying in eyes, mouth, ears, or on sensitive areas of the body. This product is not for use on wild or domestic animal bites. If you have an animal bite or puncture wound, consult your physician immediately. Do not use this product for more than ten days. If condition worsens or persists, see your physician. Do not bandage tightly. Keep this and all drugs out of reach of children. In case of accidental ingestion, seek professional assistance or contact a Poison Control Center immediately.

CONTAINS: Benzalkonium Chloride, 0.13% w/w; Alcohol 3.17%

CAUTION: Keep from freezing.

Miles Laboratories, Inc.
Consumer Products Division
Elkhart, Indiana 46515

BACTINE, Miles Laboratories, Inc., Elkhart, Indiana. Used with permission.

Questions:

1. The purpose of the spray as indicated is
    a. To cure puncture wounds.
    b. To disinfect dog bites.
    c. To heal skin wounds.
    d. To clean superficial skin wounds.

2. The maximum amount of time during which this medicine can be safely used is
    a. Indefinitely.
    b. Twenty days.
    c. Does not say.
    d. Ten days.

3. If you are bitten by an animal, according to the directions on the label you should
   a. Wash the bite with Bactine and see a doctor if it doesn't heal in ten days.
   b. Seek advice from a Poison Control Center.
   c. See your doctor immediately.

4. According to the label, Bactine can be used in three ways:
   a. To flush, spray, or remove foreign particles from a wound.
   b. To spray, invert, or remove foreign particles from a wound.
   c. To saturate, spray, or squeeze particles from a wound.

5. The recommended dosage for Bactine is
   a. 2 or 3 times a day.
   b. 10 times a day.
   c. Not indicated.

6. The term underlined superficial skin wound means
   a. A serious wound.
   b. A deep wound.
   c. A puncture wound.
   d. A minor wound.

7. According to the label, if the medicine is swallowed, you should
   a. Stay warm.
   b. Call your doctor immediately.
   c. Call the manufacturer for advice.

Answer Key:

   1. d
   2. d
   3. c
   4. a
   5. c
   6. d
   7. b

212: Cereal

Purpose: To provide practice in interpreting information found on a product label.

Introduction: In deciding what to eat you must consider whether or not your meal will include the necessary ingredients for good nutrition. Breakfast is said to be the most important meal of the day. Check to see if the following cereal will provide a wholesome breakfast.

Product Information: Quaker Whole Wheat Hot Natural Cereal

Ingredients: Rolled Whole Wheat
<u>Nutrition Information Per Serving</u>
Serving Size (⅓ cup, uncooked) .... 1 oz.
Servings per container 14

	Per 1 oz. Cereal	Per 1 oz. Cereal and ½ Cup Vitamin D Fortified Whole Milk
Calories	100	180
Protein	3g	8g
Carbohydrate	20g	26g
Fat	1g	5g

Sodium (when prepared without salt):
    Not More Than
        10mg/Serving 60mg/Serving
    Not More Than
        10mg/100g 15mg/100g

PERCENTAGE OF U.S. RECOMMENDED DAILY ALLOWANCES (% U.S. RDA)

Protein	4%	10%
Vitamin A	*	2%
Vitamin C	*	*
Thiamine	6%	8%
Riboflavin	2%	10%
Niacin	4%	4%
Calcium	*	10%
Iron	4%	4%
Vitamin D	*	10%
Phosphorus	8%	20%
Magnesium	4%	8%
Zinc	2%	6%
Copper	4%	4%

* Contains less than 2% of the U.S. RDA for this nutrient.

A 1 oz. serving of Quaker whole wheat contains about 0.5 g of fiber.

For additional nutrition information write to:
Consumer Services.

OUR GUARANTEE: Your money back if not satisfied. Just send this portion of the package along with an explanation of what you didn't like to: Consumer Services, The Quaker Oats Company, Chicago, Illinois 60654.

The Quaker Oats Company, Chicago, Illinois. Used with permission.

Questions:

1. What is the ingredient contained in Quaker Whole Wheat Hot Natural Cereal?
2. How many cups of uncooked cereal equal a 1-ounce serving?
3. How many servings of cereal can be made from one box of this cereal?
4. How many calories are contained in ½ cup of Vitamin D fortified milk?
5. What does RDA stand for?
6. When served without milk, which nutrients are less than 2% of the United States RDA?
7. When the cereal is served with ½ cup of Vitamin D fortified milk, which nutrient barely meets the RDA?
8. How many grams of fiber are contained in a 1-ounce serving of the cereal?
9. How would you obtain more information about the nutritional value of the cereal?
10. If you are not satisfied with the cereal, how would you get a refund?

Answer Key:

1. Rolled Whole Wheat
2. One-third cup
3. Fourteen
4. 80
5. Recommended Daily Allowance
6. Vitamin A, Vitamin C, Calcium, Vitamin D
7. Vitamin A
8. 0.5
9. Write to Consumer Services of the Quaker Oats Company.
10. Send guarantee portion of the box and an explanation of what was wrong with the cereal to Consumer Services, The Quaker Oats Company, Chicago, Illinois 60654.

213: Fruit Drink

Purpose: To provide practice in interpreting information found on a product label.

Introduction: To function correctly, your body must have adequate fluids. Fruit drinks are liquid and they help maintain the body's fluid level. Read this fruit drink label to learn what nutrients are contained in this drink.

Product Information:

Enriched with Vitamin C

Hi-C non-carbonated fruit drinks are made with real fruit juice. Serve at breakfast, with other meals, or at any other time during the day.

Chill, Shake and Serve

NUTRITION INFORMATION PER SERVING

SERVING SIZE	6 FL. OZ.
SERVINGS PER CONTAINER	7⅔
CALORIC CONTENT	90
PROTEIN CONTENT	0 GMS.
CARBOHYDRATE CONTENT	23 GMS.
FAT CONTENT	0 GMS.

PERCENTAGE OF U.S. RECOMMENDED DAILY ALLOWANCE (U.S. RDA)

VITAMIN C 100%
CONTAINS LESS THAN 2% OF THE U.S. RDA OF PROTEIN, VITAMIN A, THIAMINE, RIBOFLAVIN, NIACIN, CALCIUM, AND IRON.

CONTAINS WATER, SUGAR AND CORN SWEETENERS, CONCENTRATED ORANGE JUICE, FUMARIC, CITRIC AND MALIC ACIDS (PROVIDE TARTNESS), SODIUM CITRATE (CONTROLS ACIDITY), NATURAL FLAVORS, VITAMIN C, ARTIFICIAL COLOR.
CONTAINS 10% ORANGE JUICE

Refrigerate after opening

46 fl. oz. (1.36 liters)

DISTRIBUTED BY K

The Coca-Cola Company
FOODS DIVISION
HOUSTON TEXAS 77001 U.S.A.

HI-C is a registered trademark of The Coca-Cola Company. Used with permission.

Questions:

1. The label says "made with real fruit juice." How much real fruit juice is contained in this orange drink?
2. After the container has been opened, where must this drink be stored?
3. The label says the drink is enriched with Vitamin C. What percentage of the RDA is contained in this drink?
4. What ingredients make the drink taste tart?
5. How do you know that this drink is not made in the same way as soda?
6. This drink is manufactured by what soft drink company?

Answer Key:

1. 10%
2. Refrigerator
3. 100%
4. Citric and malic acids
5. It is non-carbonated
6. The Coca-Cola Company

214: Bleach

Purpose: To provide practice in interpreting information found on a product label.

Introduction: Your home contains many household items that are designed to help you with your daily chores. If used incorrectly, however, these items can be very harmful. Read the following label to learn about a common household item, bleach.

Product Information:

YOUR LAUNDRY NEEDS CLOROX BLEACH.

For the broad range of laundry problems you encounter, no other type of additive used with your detergent can give a cleaner, brighter looking wash. And Clorox disinfects, too.

DIRECTIONS FOR USE

HOW MUCH CLOROX SHOULD YOU USE?

To get the best cleaning results, you should use the proper amount of Clorox in the wash water. If too little is used, stubborn dirt and stains that detergent alone cannot remove may be left in and whites and colored fabrics may not stay as white and bright as possible.

The guidelines below should provide excellent cleaning results with any good soap or detergent. However, if you wash extremely heavily soiled or very large loads, you may want to add slightly more Clorox.

● Large top-loading automatic...1-1/2 cups
● Regular top-loading automatic.....1 cup
● Front-loading automatic........1/2 cup
● Heavily soiled laundry—
    increase amount above by.....1/4 cup
● Hand laundry—
    2 gallons of sudsy water.......1/8 cup

WHAT FABRICS CAN YOU BLEACH?

Cotton, linen, synthetics (including 100% polyester and polyester/cotton blends), permanent press and most colored fabrics can be safely bleached. In fact, approximately 75% of today's colored garments that have "Do Not Bleach" care labels are actually bleach-safe. You can test any article to determine if it is bleach-safe by applying one drop of a test solution (1 tablespoon of Clorox with 1/4 cup of water) to a hidden part of the fabric. Be sure to check all colors including trim. Let stand 1 minute, then blot dry. If there is no color change the article can be safely bleached. Do not use Clorox on silk, wool, mohair, leather, spandex, or non-fast colors. Repeated use on flame-retardant fabrics made of 100% cotton may cause loss of flame retardancy.

HOW SHOULD YOU ADD CLOROX TO YOUR WASHLOAD?

Select the way to add Clorox that is easiest for you: in the wash water before the laundry is put in, or diluted with a quart of water after the washer has begun agitating. For a washer with automatic bleach dispenser, follow the manufacturer's instructions.

WHAT SPECIAL LAUNDRY PROBLEMS CAN CLOROX HELP SOLVE?

Diapers, baby clothes, and children's bedcovers can be cleaned by following the regular Clorox laundry instructions. Washing with Clorox will remove stains, eliminate most germs, and tend to reduce diaper irritation. Clorox is an excellent disinfectant and deodorizer, yet is economical to use. However, repeated use on flame-retardant sleepwear made of 100% cotton may cause loss of flame retardancy.

CAUTION: Clorox may be harmful if swallowed or may cause severe eye irritation if splashed in eyes. If swallowed, feed milk. If splashed in eyes, flood with water. Call physician. Skin irritant; if contact with skin, wash off with water.
● Do not use Clorox with ammonia or products containing acids such as toilet bowl cleaners, rust removers or vinegar. To do so will release hazardous gases. Prolonged contact with metal may cause pitting or discoloration. Do not use this bottle for storage of any other liquid but Clorox.

©1980 THE CLOROX COMPANY, OAKLAND, CA 94612 MADE IN U.S.A. EPA REG. NO. 5813-1
CLOROX is a registered trademark of The Clorox Company

CLOROX BLEACH, The Clorox Company, Oakland, California. Used with permission.

Questions:

1. To achieve the best cleaning results when doing laundry, bleach is used in the washing machine in addition to what other product?

2. Using the proper amount of bleach in the washing machine is very important. How much bleach should be used in a regular top-loading automatic with heavily soiled clothes?

3. What percentage of the clothes labeled "Do Not Bleach" can actually be safely bleached?

4. What type of flame retardant fabric may lose its flame retardancy after repeated washing in bleach?

5. If you accidentally splash bleach in your eye, what first aid procedures should you follow?

6. Bleach can be hazardous to your health if it is used in combination with what other products? Why?

7. With what types of materials can you never use bleach?

Answer Key:

1. Soap or detergent

2. 1 and ¼ cups

3. 75%

4. 100% cotton

5. Flood eye with water and call physician

6. Ammonia or products containing acids such as toilet bowl cleaners, rust removers, or vinegar; hazardous gases are released

7. Silk, wool, mohair, leather, spandex, and non-fast colors

215: Disinfectant

Purpose: To provide practice in interpreting information found on a product label.

Introduction: Disinfectants are used to kill germs that cause disease. Read the following label to learn how this disinfectant should be used.

Product Information: DISINFECT-ALL

Hospital-Proven General Use Disinfectant

Always use DISINFECT-ALL for cleaning throughout your home! Get rid of disease germs everywhere! Cleans bathrooms, kitchens, garbage pails, sick rooms, floors, walls, woodwork, kennels, and cellars.

DISINFECT-ALL kills a wider variety of disease-producing germs than do other products such as pine oils or bleaches. Don't risk disease from germs other products cannot kill.

DIRECTIONS FOR USE: For general household cleaning, add 1 tablespoon DISINFECT-ALL to 1 quart of water. To kill many viruses and bacteria, increase amount of DISINFECT-ALL to 2 tablespoons per 1 quart water. When cleaning a sick room, increase amount of DISINFECT-ALL to 4 tablespoons per 1 quart water to kill more powerful germs such as "staph."

WONDERFUL FOR YOUR DOG, TOO! Bathe your dog in water to which has been added 3 tablespoons of DISINFECT-ALL per gallon of water. This will remove odors and fleas and keep your dog's coat sleek and glossy. Avoid contact with eyes.

Questions:

1. What institution has used this disinfectant and proved it to be safe and effective?
2. What other types of disinfectants are identified on the label?
3. What types of germs does the label say are killed by DISINFECT-ALL?
4. If you are disinfecting an area where a sick person has been, how many tablespoons of DISINFECT-ALL should be used with each quart of water?
5. When DISINFECT-ALL is used in your dog's bath water, you must be careful not to get the water on what part of the dog?

Answer Key:

1 Hospital
2. Pine oils and bleaches
3. Viruses, bacteria, staph
4. Four
5. His eyes

ACTIVITIES FOR FOLLOWING DIRECTIONS

The following nine activities are designed to help your students understand how to follow directions that may appear in everyday situations. Directions are important in knowing how to use the telephone directory, following first aid procedures, and operating a fire extinguisher. Also included are examples that illustrate everyday life skills such as following washing instructions on garment labels, following a recipe in a cookbook, preparing frozen foods, and assembling a toy.

Materials for these activities may be used individually or by small groups of students. You may also use these activities as the basis for a lesson with the entire class in which you print the directions on the chalkboard, read the questions aloud, and have the students answer aloud.

216: Telephone Directory Information

Purpose: To provide practice in reading and interpreting information found in the telephone directory.

Introduction: When you use a telephone, it is important to know how to use the telephone directory to locate service numbers, such as Directory Assistance, and other information regarding telephone company services. One section that contains this type of information is the "Service and Other Calls" section in the front of the telephone directory. Study the following listing of telephone numbers and answer the questions that follow.

Directions:

SERVICE AND OTHER CALLS

BUSINESS OFFICE - Residence Telephone Service......................dial 396-9101
    Billing Information, Business Transactions,
    New Service, Termination or Suspension of Service
    Office Hours - 8:30 A.M. to 5 P.M.
          Monday through Friday
    From telephones beginning with   dial
      653, 655.................................488-5511
      881, 882, 884, 885........................566-7155
      892.......................................488-5511

REPAIR SERVICE - 24 hour .... dial 611
    Out of Order Telephones and Other Telephone Repairs

ASSISTANCE IN CALLING .... dial "OPERATOR"

DIRECTORY ASSISTANCE
    412 Area
      653, 655 Telephones.........................dial 1 + 555-1212
          (chargeable after exceeding the call allowance)
    All Other Telephones........................dial 555-1212
    Outside 412 Area
      653, 655 Telephones...................dial 1 + Area Code + 555-1212
    All Other Telephones..................dial Area Code + 555-1212
          (no charge for these calls)

The Bell Telephone Company of Pennsylvania. Used with permission.

Questions:
1. How many hours a day is the business office open?
    a. 8 hours   c. 8 and 1/2 hours
    b. 7 hours   d. 7 and 1/2 hours

2. If you lived in an area where your telephone number began with 884, what number would you call if you had a question about your monthly telephone bill?
    a. 396-9101   c. 566-7155
    b. 0   d. 555-1212

3. When your telephone is not working properly, what number would you call to report the problem?
    a. 566-7155   c. 0
    b. 611   d. 396-9101

4. If your telephone number begins with 882 and you do not know the telephone number for a friend living in the 412 area, what number would you dial for assistance?
    a. 555-1212   c. 0
    b. 1-555-1212   d. Area Code + 555-1212

Answer Key:

   1. c   2. c   3. b   4. a

217: Telephone Control

Purpose: To provide practice in reading and interpreting information found in the telephone directory.

Introduction: The types of phone calls made on a telephone are regulated by law. Phone calls that are made to harass, annoy, etc. are illegal. Read the information in the following excerpt from a telephone directory and learn about the regulations that are imposed for your safety and protection. Answer the questions that follow.

Directions:

warning: EMERGENCY CALLS ON PARTY LINES, OBSCENE OR INDECENT LANGUAGE AND ANONYMOUS CALLS

Federal Law and the Crimes Code of Pennsylvania provide:

It is unlawful for anyone to use the telephone in making an intrastate, interstate, or foreign communication as a means of conveying obscene or indecent language or to telephone anonymously another person repeatedly for the purpose of annoying, molesting, or harassing such person or his or her family. Such offense is punishable by fine or imprisonment or both.

In addition, the Crimes Code of Pennsylvania provides:

Any person who willfully refuses to relinquish immediately a party line when informed that it is needed for an emergency call to a fire department, a police department, or for medical aid or ambulance service, is guilty of an offense and subject to fine or imprisonment or both. The statute defines an "emergency" as a situation in which property or human life are in jeopardy and the prompt summoning of aid is essential. It is also made an offense subject to the same penalties to obtain the use of a party line by falsely stating that it is needed for such an emergency call.

Anyone with intent to defraud, who gives information to the operator or agent of any telephone company, so that the charge therefore is made to the account of another without authorization, shall be liable to fine or imprisonment or both.

The Bell Telephone Company of Pennsylvania. Used with permission.

Questions:

1. This warning information was meant to be used in what state?

2. If a person is caught making obscene or indecent telephone calls, what punishment can he receive?

3. If an emergency arises and you must contact a person whose telephone number registers a busy signal, how could you contact him?

4. What four types of offenses listed in this warning are punishable by a fine or imprisonment?

Answer Key:

1. Pennsylvania.

2. Fine, imprisonment, or both.

3. Call the operator and say that you have an emergency.

4. Making offensive telephone calls, refusing to give up the line for an emergency, falsely claiming that you need to make an emergency call, charging a call to someone else's account without authorization.

218: Classified Telephone Directory

Purpose: To provide practice in reading and interpreting information found in the classified telephone directory.

Introduction: An important supplement to your telephone directory is the classified section. These pages help you locate places of business for home and personal buying needs.

Bring a classified telephone directory to class. Read the questions listed below and use the classified directory to answer them.

Questions:

1. If you were ill and needed to see a doctor, list an address where one could be found.

2. Your home water heater has started to leak. What type of serviceman would you call? On what pages of the directory can you find all of these repairmen listed?

3. If you were looking for a new Ford automobile, what dealers could you visit? List two that are closest to your school. What are their telephone numbers?

4. What number could you call to place an advertisement in the classified directory?

5. List a telephone number for each of the following:

Police Department	Your School
Fire Department	Optician
Taxi Cab Company	Hospital

Answer Key:

Answers will vary.

219: First Aid for Frostbite

Purpose: To provide practice in following and interpreting directions found in a first aid manual.

Introduction: In an emergency situation, your knowledge of first aid procedures can be very valuable. If a person is injured and needs help, you may need to administer first aid until a doctor can be summoned. One way of knowing what to do is to read the instructions contained in a first aid manual. Your ability to follow the directions may save a person much discomfort.

Read the following directions for the treatment of frostbite, and on a separate sheet of paper answer the questions that follow.

Directions: TREATMENT OF FROSTBITE INFORMATION

The areas of the body most commonly affected by freezing are the nose, toes, fingers, and ears. Frozen tissue can be recognized by its white color. As soon as a person is found to have frostbite, he should be removed from the freezing temperature. To treat the damaged area, you should attempt to rapidly thaw the frozen areas. Rapid rewarming should be done in water at a temperature of 111 or 112 degrees Fahrenheit with circulating water. The thawing tissue must not be massaged because massaging can result in tissue damage. After the tissue is thawed, keep the person warm but do not apply direct heat to the thawed areas. Applying direct heat increases the cell activity and can result in tissue damage. If, after you have completed this process, the person still complains of pain or numbness, immediately take him to a doctor.

Questions:

1. What areas of the body are most commonly affected by frostbite?
2. What color is flesh that is suffering from frostbite?
3. What is the first thing you should do when you discover a person who has frostbite?
4. When you treat frostbite, should you warm the affected area rapidly or slowly?
5. The water used to warm the affected tissue should be how warm?
6. After the affected area is thawed, should you stimulate the area by massaging it? Why or why not?
7. After the tissue is thawed, is it a good idea to place the affected area on a heating pad? Why or why not?
8. When should a doctor be consulted?

Answer Key:

1. Nose, toes, fingers, and ears.

2. White.

3. Get him out of the cold.

4. Rapidly.

5. 111 or 112 degrees Fahrenheit.

6. No. Can result in tissue damage.

7. No. Direct heat can cause tissue damage.

8. If you have followed these directions and pain or numbness still persists

220: Fire Extinguisher Information

Purpose: To provide practice in reading and interpreting information found on a fire extinguisher.

Introduction: Fire extinguishers are found in all school buildings. They are placed there for your protection and to help extinguish small fires that might erupt. They are designed to extinguish specific types of fires, and they extinguish these fires best if used in the manner specified in the directions for their use. Read the following directions that are found on one type of fire extinguisher and learn about its intended use.

Directions: FIRE EXTINGUISHER INFORMATION

The U.L. listed Tornado Challenger 1202 (BCF) fire extinguishers have been carefully designed to fight fires and they are recommended for use against the following types of fires:

Class A   Carbonaceous Fires
Class B   Flammable Liquid Fires
Class C   Electrical Fires

OPERATION: To operate the extinguisher, remove it from its bracket or wall hook, hold it upright by the handgrip, with the right hand at convenient arm's length. Pull out the safety pin which is indicated by the silver disc. Holding the hose in the left hand, direct the spray nozzle toward the base of the fire source. Then squeeze the lever on the handgrip hard using the palm of the right hand. When you squeeze this lever, a green indicator square is ejected from the rear of the extinguisher, and extinguishant is released from the spray nozzle in a conical pattern. Maximum extinguishing effect is obtained if you keep moving in towards the base of the fire source as it is extinguished.

CAUTION:

CONTENTS UNDER PRESSURE. Protect from corrosive conditions; if there is any corrosion or damage, extinguisher should be carefully emptied and discarded.

Use only as directed. Do not incinerate.

Questions:

1. What three types of fires can be extinguished by this fire extinguisher?
2. How far out in front of you should you hold the extinguisher when you use it?
3. What indicates where the safety pin is located?
4. When you are extinguishing a fire, toward what part of the fire should you direct the spray?
5. Which hand is used to depress the trigger that allows the extinguishant to be released?
6. Why should you move in toward the fire as you are using the fire extinguisher?
7. If the extinguisher becomes corroded, what should you do before you dispose of it? Why?
8. Why can you not dispose of the extinguisher by throwing it in a fire?

Answer Key:

1. Carbonaceous Fires, Flammable Liquid Fires, and Electrical Fires.
2. At arm's length.
3. Silver disc.
4. Base.
5. Right hand.
6. You will be able to accurately direct the extinguishant to the base of the fire and you will achieve the maximum amount of effect.
7. Empty it. It might explode or in some other way injure a person.
8. Because it is pressurized and will explode

221: Laundering Instructions

Purpose: To provide practice in reading and interpreting directions for laundering found on garment labels.

Introduction: Recent consumer legislation has required clothing manufacturers to supply laundering instructions on garments. The variety of synthetic fabrics available today makes this type of information a necessity. Because an incorrectly laundered garment can be permanently damaged, it is essential that the directions on the labels are read and followed correctly.

Read the laundering instructions for three garments listed below and answer the questions that follow.

Directions: GARMENT 1   Hand Washable in Warm Water
Use Mild Soap
Squeeze Gently
Do Not Use Bleach
Do Not Twist or Wring

GARMENT 2   Machine Wash
Warm Setting
Gentle Cycle
Use bleach on whites only
Wash deep solid colors separately
Tumble Dry
Remove promptly
If pressed, use warm iron

GARMENT 3   Machine Wash
Warm Water
Tumble Dry at Low Temp or Drip Dry
Use Cool Iron to Touch Up if Needed

Questions:

Garment 1

1. Should this garment be washed in an automatic washer?

2. Which of the following soap powders would be best for washing this garment—Ivory Snow, Tide, Cold Power?

3. How should you remove excess moisture from the garment after washing it by hand?

4. Why do you think the directions included "Do not twist or wring"?

Garment 2

5. What washing machine settings are recommended for this garment?

6. If the label is found on a white blouse, is it safe to use bleach?

7. What special care would be required if this label were on a navy blue blouse? Why?

8. Why should the garment be removed promptly from the drier?

Garment 3

9. What water temperature is recommended for this garment?

10. What methods of drying are recommended?

11. What does "Drip Dry" mean?

12. Is it likely that this garment will need to be ironed?

Answer Key:

1. No.

2. Ivory Snow.

3. Squeeze gently.

4. Probably will set wrinkles in the fabric while wet.

5. Warm water, gentle cycle.

6. Yes.

7. Wash separately because the color will fade.

8. To prevent wrinkling.

9. Warm.

10. Machine drying or drip dry.

11. Hanging the garment on a clothesline while still wet.

12. No (touch up if needed)

222: Recipe

Purpose: To provide practice in reading and interpreting directions found in a recipe

Introduction: No recipe, no matter how good, can give the desired results, unless you read and follow the directions with utmost care. It is a good idea to read the entire recipe through first to become completely familiar with it. Then read it again, making note of the necessary ingredients and preparations. Timing is also an important part of food preparation. Be sure to allow enough time, not only to cook the food, but also to prepare the ingredients.

Read the following recipe for a tuna casserole and then answer the questions that follow.

Directions: SOUPER TUNA CASSEROLE

1 8 oz. box elbow macaroni
1 6½ oz. can tuna (drained, rinsed, and flaked)
1 4½ oz. jar sliced mushrooms (do not drain)
1 8½ oz. can young peas (drained)
1 11 oz. can cheddar cheese soup (undiluted)
¼ cup milk

1 cup crushed potato chips for topping (optional)

Cook macaroni as label directs. Drain and rinse the cooked macaroni.

Preheat oven to 350°. Lightly grease a 2-quart casserole dish.

Combine cooked macaroni with soup, mushrooms, peas, tuna, and milk. Gently toss until ingredients are well mixed. Sprinkle with crushed potato chips if desired.

Bake at 350° for 40 minutes or until cheese sauce is hot and bubbly. Serves 6.

Questions:

1. If the label on the macaroni directs you to "Boil 7 to 12 minutes; boil only 6 to 7 minutes when using in a casserole where it will receive further cooking," how long would you boil the macaroni for use in this recipe?
2. What does <u>undiluted</u> mean in the list of ingredients after the soup?
3. What special preparations are required for the tuna?
4. What part of the recipe can be omitted if you wish?
5. What size dish is recommended? If you did not have this exact size, would you choose a smaller or larger size that you did have?
6. What oven temperature is given for baking the casserole?
7. How can you tell when the casserole is ready to serve?
8. Would this recipe serve six people if each had a second helping?
9. Would 40 minutes be sufficient time in which to prepare this casserole?

Answer Key:

1. 6 to 7 minutes.
2. The soup just as it comes out of the can with no water added.
3. The tuna must be drained, rinsed in cold water, and separated into flakes with a fork.
4. The crushed potato chip topping.
5. 2-quart; larger.
6. 350 degrees.
7. The cheese sauce is hot and bubbly.
8. No. "Serves 6" means six servings; this recipe would serve three people if each had a second helping.
9. No; requires baking time of 35 minutes plus boiling time for the macaroni (6 to 7 minutes) and time to prepare and combine all the ingredients.

223: Preparing Frozen Food

Purpose: To provide practice in reading and interpreting directions found on a frozen food package.

Introduction: To take full advantage of the convenience of frozen foods, you must be able to read and follow the directions printed on the package. When you prepare frozen food, best results will be obtained by following the cooking instructions exactly as given.

Read the directions below and answer the questions that follow.

Directions: COOKING INSTRUCTIONS FOR FROZEN PEAS

Cooking Instructions:

1. Put unopened pouch into boiling water in uncovered pan.
2. Bring water to second boil. Cook about 15 minutes.
3. Tear or cut open pouch at side notch; pour into bowl. Stir and serve.

Microwave Cooking Instructions:

1. Make a small slit in center of pouch and place in oven.
2. Microwave about 6 to 7 minutes. (Allow more time for additional pouches.)
3. Tear or cut open pouch at side notch; pour into bowl. Stir and serve.

Helpful Hints for Variety

For flavorful variety, cook according to package directions and try one of the following hints:

- Stir in 1/3 cup bias-cut celery sautéed with one 2½ oz. jar whole mushrooms, drained; 1/2 tsp. basil leaves, crushed.
- Stir in 2 tbsp. hickory smoke flavored process cheese spread; 1 tsp. chopped chives.
- Sprinkle with 3 tbsp. crushed seasoned croutons.

Questions:

1. When cooking the peas, you are directed to place the cooking pouch into a pan of water. When should you place the pouch into the water?
2. The instructions say to bring the water to a second boil. What does this mean?
3. How long do you cook the peas in the boiling water?
4. If you have a microwave oven, what must you do to the pouch before you place it in the oven?
5. How long do you cook the peas in the microwave oven?
6. Why does the manufacturer provide the "Helpful Hints" section?

Answer Key:

1. After bringing the water to a boil.
2. When the pouch is placed into the boiling water, the water will stop boiling. You must let the water return to boil a second time before starting the recommended 15 minutes cooking time.

3. 15 minutes.

4. Make a small slit in the center of the pouch.

5. 6 to 7 minutes.

6. To help you add variety to your meals.

224: Assembling a Model Car

Purpose: To provide practice in reading and interpreting directions for assembling a model car.

Introduction: If you want to build model cars, you will need to be able to follow directions. Included below are sample directions from a model car kit. Read the directions for assembling the model and answer the questions that follow.

Directions: IMPORTANT DIRECTIONS! READ THIS INFORMATION BEFORE YOU BEGIN WORKING ON THE MODEL.

1. **Before snapping parts together, trim excess plastic from parts.**

2. **Snap parts together carefully. Once the parts have been snapped together they cannot be disassembled without doing damage to the individual parts.**

3. **Painting the model is optional. If you do decide to paint your model, be sure to use bottle or spray paint made for styrene plastic.**

4. **To apply decals to unpainted assembled model, wash the model with warm, soapy water before putting the decals in place.**

Questions:

1. Before assembling the model, what is the first thing you must do?

2. Will you need glue to assemble this kit?

3. You must be careful when you assemble the model. Because of the assembly procedure, what might happen if you attempted to disconnect pieces that are already assembled?

4. To insure that the decals will stick to the unpainted model, what must you do to prepare the surface?

5. Can this model be painted? If so, what type of paint is recommended?

Answer Key:

1. Trim excess plastic from parts.

2. No; parts snap together.

3. Might be damaged or broken.

4. Wash the model with warm, soapy water.

5. Yes. Bottle or spray paint made for styrene plastic.

ACTIVITIES FOR LOCATING AND USING REFERENCES

The following ten activities are designed to help your students locate and use reference materials. All materials included in this section, with the possible exception of map-reading, give the student practice in locating and using reference materials in books, magazines, newspapers, and the library. Exercises are included for interpreting and using a table of contents, indexes in a book and newspaper, a dictionary, an encyclopedia, and the *Readers' Guide to Periodical Literature*.

The activities listed on the following pages were designed to be used by one student at a time. You can increase the number of activities for each area by creating exercises and questions of your own. The exercises included will be even more meaningful if they are preceded by a trip to the school library and a lesson taught by you or the librarian on each of the topics. By using exercises such as these, your students will be better prepared to locate and efficiently use reference materials.

225: Table of Contents

Purpose: To provide practice in using information found in a table of contents.

Introduction: To help you locate specific information in a book or magazine, a table of contents is included at the front of the book or magazine. The table of contents lists the chapter titles, headings, subheadings, etc. in the order in which they appear in the book, and gives the page numbers for each. Similarly, in a magazine, the table of contents lists the articles found in that particular issue and gives the page numbers.

Included below is a sample table of contents from a magazine. Read the information given, and on a separate sheet of paper answer the questions that follow.

Reference Material:

Care for Your Dog Vol. 20, No. 5 April 1985

Table of Contents:

Care of the Christmas Puppy 1
Basic Training Principles 5
Children and Animal Care 8
Canadian Canines 10
The Fight Against Fleas 11

Questions:

1. What is the name of the magazine?

2. On what page would you find the article "The Fight Against Fleas"?

3. How many pages long is the article entitled "Basic Training Principles"?

4. Which article is the longest?

5. Which article would tell you about dogs in another country?

6. Which articles tell about showing dogs?

7. If you had a problem dog, on what pages would you find helpful information?

8. Page 20 would contain information from what article?

9. If you gave a friend a dog for Christmas, what article would be appropriate for him to read?

10. What type of information is discussed in this magazine?

Answer Key:

1. Care for Your Dog

2. 11

3. 3

4. "The Fight Against Fleas"

5. "Canadian Canines"

6. "How to Show Your Dog" and "Junior Showmanship"

7. 5-7

8. "Intestinal Parasites in Dogs"

9. "Care of the Christmas Puppy"

10. Information on dogs

226: The Card Catalog

Purpose: To provide practice in identifying author, title, and subject cards in the card catalog.

Introduction: When you are trying to locate a book in a library, the card catalog is the first place you should check. The card catalog contains file cards arranged in alphabetical order. These cards represent all the books in the library—fiction and nonfiction. Each work of fiction is represented by two cards in the card catalog: an author card and a title card. If, for example, you wanted to see if the school library has a copy of *Treasure Island* by Robert Louis Stevenson, you could look either in the "S" section of the card catalog for the author card for Stevenson or in the "T" section for the title card for *Treasure Island*. Similarly, each nonfiction book is represented in the card catalog by an author card and a title card, but it also has cards filed under subject heading(s). If you do not know the author or title of a book on a specific topic (such as "Motorcycles"), then you can look alphabetically in the card catalog for the subject heading and find listed all the books in the library on that subject.

Reference Material: Listed below are author, title, and subject headings as they would appear in the library's card catalog.

1. DOGS	6. White Fang
2. London, Jack	7. FOLK SONGS
3. Black Stallion	8. Dickens, Charles
4. Sewell, Anna	9. BASEBALL
5. Little Women	10. INDIANS

Questions:

1. Of the ten headings listed above, which are subject headings?

2. *Black Stallion*, *Little Women*, and *White Fang* are what type of card catalog entry?

3. List the three author entries.

Answer Key:

1. DOGS, FOLK SONGS, BASEBALL, INDIANS

2. Title

3 London, Jack
   Sewell, Anna
   Dickens, Charles

227: The Card Catalog

Purpose: To provide practice in interpreting information found on a card in the card catalog.

Introduction: The card catalog contains three types of cards: author, title, and subject. Once you have located a card for a book that interests you, you must be able to interpret the information on the card so that you will be able to locate the book on the library shelf. Each card catalog card contains the following information about the book: name of author, call number, title of the book, publisher and date of publication, and number of pages.

Look at the sample author card given below. Read the questions that follow the card and answer them on a separate sheet of paper.

Reference Material:

F208 W	Wood, Michael Lee. Sea and Sunshine, the Southern Coastal States: Florida, Georgia, North Carolina, South Carolina, Virginia. Illustrated by Jay Kelsel. McGraw-Hill Pub. Inc. (1975). 102p illus 24cm 1. Southern States--Descr. & Travel--Juvenile Lit.

Questions:

1. The title of the book listed is
   a. The Southern States
   b. Sea and Sunshine
   c. Southern Coastal States

2. The number of pages in the book is
   a. 24
   b. 122
   c. 102

3. The artist who drew the pictures for the book is
   a. Michael Wood
   b. Jay Kelsel
   c. Not Given

4. What type of information is included in the book?
   a. Descriptions and travel information
   b. Listing of sea adventures
   c. Description of the sun and the sea

5. The type of reader that this book is written for is
   a. Adult
   b. College or older
   c. Teenager or younger

Answer Key:

   1. b
   2. c
   3. b
   4. a
   5. c

228: Dictionary

Purpose: To provide practice in using information found in a dictionary.

Introduction: When you use a dictionary, you should be aware of all the information that it contains. In addition to words and their definitions, many dictionaries also contain supplementary lists, charts, and guides.

Listed below are some examples of the sections found in many dictionaries. Study the list and on a separate sheet of paper answer the questions that follow.

Reference Material: SPECIAL FEATURES OF A DICTIONARY

A Guide to Pronunciation
Biographical Names
Abbreviations and Symbols of Chemical Elements
Abbreviations Used in This Work
Proofreaders' Marks
A Pronouncing Gazetteer
Colleges and Universities in the United States and
  Canada
Spelling
A Pronouncing Vocabulary of Common English Given
  Names
Vocabulary of Rhymes

Questions:

1. What is the name of the section that explains how to pronounce words that are found in the dictionary?
2. Which section lists abbreviations that are used in the dictionary?
3. Which section lists marks used in correcting manuscripts?
4. Which section lists short forms of words and symbols of chemical elements?
5. Which section lists dates, nationality, and status or occupation of the persons included?
6. Which section gives basic information about the countries of the world and their most important regions, cities, and natural features?
7. Which section lists proper names that are most frequently used in the English language?
8. Which section includes all institutions of higher education in the United States?
9. Which section contains rules of spelling?
10. Which section lists rhymes by their sounds?

Answer Key:
1. A Guide to Pronunciation
2. Abbreviations Used in This Work
3. Proofreaders' Marks
4. Abbreviations and Symbols of Chemical Elements
5. Biographical Names
6. A Pronouncing Gazetteer
7. A Pronouncing Vocabulary of Common English Given Names
8. Colleges and Universities in the United States and Canada
9. Spelling
10. Vocabulary of Rhymes

229: Dictionary

Purpose: To provide practice in learning how to find a word in a dictionary.

Introduction: Two skills that are very important when you use a dictionary are alphabetizing and using guide words. Because words in a dictionary are listed in alphabetical order, your skill in alphabetizing will enable you to locate words more easily and more quickly. Knowing how to use guide words correctly will also help you to locate words in a dictionary. The guide words are printed in heavy type at the top of each dictionary page. The guide word on the left is the same word as the <u>first</u> word on the page, and the guide word on the right is the same word as the <u>last</u> word on the page. Words that fall alphabetically between the guide words will be on that page. By scanning the guide words as you turn the pages of a dictionary, you can locate the exact page on which a word will appear.

The following two exercises will provide practice for you in alphabetizing and using guide words.

Exercise 1. Arrange the words listed below in the correct alphabetical order. If the first letters are the same, you will have to use the second, third, or fourth letters to place the words in correct order.

1. deflate	6. change
2. close	7. club
3. bowl	8. defer
4. automobile	9. bend
5. bracket	10. awake

Exercise 2. Listed below are four sets of guide words and sixteen words that would be found alphabetized under them in a dictionary. Write the words in alphabetical order under the guide words where they would be found.

Guide Words   buckle-bugle   deflected-deity
           gadget-gall   sackful-safety

Words

1. bug	5. bucksaw	9. sad	13. degree
2. deil	6. deform	10. gain	14. buff
3. galaxy	7. gage	11. defray	15. gait
4. sadness	8. sacred	12. buddle	16. saddle

Answer Key:

Exercise 1

1. automobile	6. change
2. awake	7. close
3. bend	8. club
4. bowl	9. defer
5. bracket	10. deflate

Exercise 2

buckle-bugle   deflected-deity

1. bucksaw	1. deform
2. buddle	2. defray
3. buff	3. degree
4. bug	4. deil

gadget-gall   sackful-safety

1. gage	1. sacred
2. gain	2. sad
3. gait	3. saddle
4. galaxy	4. sadness

230: Index

Purpose: To provide practice in using information found in an index.

Introduction: Magazines, newspapers, books, and other printed sources often have an index. An index is used to help people locate information and the page on which it appears. The subject headings or topics are usually arranged in alphabetical order.

Included below is a sample of an index from a newspaper. Read the information contained in the index and on a separate sheet of paper answer the questions that follow.

Reference Material: INDEX

SUPPLEMENTS

Family Magazine, TV Graphic, Roto, Parade, Comics

AD SECTIONS

Gimbels, K Mart, Murphy's Mart, Radio Shack

PRESS PHONES

Delivery 555-2121
Want Ads 555-2014
Other Depts 555-1106

Questions:

1. Where would you find information on new and interesting recipes?

2. What are the supplemental sections that will come with your newspaper?

3. If you were looking for a job, under which section of the newspaper would you look?

4. In what section and on what page would you find information about the weather?

5. How many sections does this newspaper have?

6. Which of the entries in the index represents the longest section in the newspaper?

7. Under which section of the index would you look to find the following topics:

   a. Old furniture
   b. Baseball scores
   c. Winter vacation spots
   d. Home prices
   e. Best Seller List
   f. Weather
   g. Designs of new clothes
   h. Letters from readers

Answer Key:

1. Press Chef E8

2. Family Magazine, TV Graphic, Roto, Parade, Comics

3. Want Ads C3-29

4. Section A, Page 19

5. Seven (A to G)

6. Want Ads

7. a. Antiques
   b. Sports News
   c. Travel/Resorts
   d. Real Estate
   e. Book Reviews
   f. Weather Map
   g. Fashions
   h. Letters to Editor

231: Index

Purpose: To provide practice in using information found in an index

Introduction: To find information in some indexes, you will have to use what is called "cross indexing." When an index contains "cross indexing," you may have to turn to a different section of the index to find the page where your information is located.

Study the sample index given below. Then read the questions that follow and refer to the sample index to find the answers. Write your answers on a separate sheet of paper.

Reference Material:

INDEX

Questions:

1. Where would you find information about junkyards?

2. If you were interested in attending a car auction, where would you look to find information?

3. Under what three headings could you find information on borrowing money to purchase a car?

4. On what page could you find information about lacquer paint manufacturers?

5. If you wished to purchase a rebuilt part for your car, what page would list the dealers that you should contact?

Answer Key:

1. Automobile Parts & Supplies—Used & Rebuilt
   Junk Dealers
2. Automobile Auctions, Page 70
3. Banks, Financing, Loans
4. Page 580
5. Page 111

232: Encyclopedia

Purpose: To provide practice in finding information in an encyclopedia.

Introduction: An encyclopedia is a comprehensive reference source that can be useful at home, at school, or in a library. Encyclopedias cover a wide range of topics under specific headings arranged in alphabetical order. Encyclopedias include lengthy articles on large subjects. Information about persons, places, and events and facts that are of interest and importance to a large number of people are included in encyclopedias.

An encyclopedia may be a single volume (such as a desk encyclopedia) but more often an encyclopedia is a set of volumes. Multivolume encyclopedia sets are arranged according to two systems: unit-letter arrangement and split-letter arrangement. In unit-letter arrangement, there is a volume for each letter of the alphabet (Volume A, Volume B, etc.). Some letters may be combined such as Volume X-Y-Z. In split-letter arrangement, the volumes are divided more evenly according to the amount of information. Volumes in this arrangement are not labeled according to any set pattern; for example, the first three volumes might be "A to ANNO", "ANNU to BALTIC", "BALTIM to BRAIL."

The following two exercises will provide practice for you in using an encyclopedia to locate information.

Exercise 1. Which of the following questions would be most likely to be answered in an encyclopedia? On a separate sheet of paper number from 1 to 8. Read each question and if you think the answer to the question can be found in an encyclopedia, place an "X" beside the corresponding number on your answer sheet.

1. Who discovered a vaccine for polio?
2. What was the most popular television program in 1979?
3. Who was Prime Minister of England during World War II?
4. Who was the most valuable player in Super Bowl XIII?
5. Which horse won the Kentucky Derby in 1979?
6. How does a kidney function?
7. How do ants build their homes?
8. What Indian tribes were located in North Dakota?

Exercise 2. Written below are the letters for four volumes of a split-letter encyclopedia set and a list of subjects. Read the subject headings and decide in which volume each would appear. Write the number of the encyclopedia volume (1, 2, 3, or 4) on your answer sheet.

Volume 1 GUNN-HYDROX
Volume 2 HYDROX-JEREM
Volume 3 JEREZ-LIBE
Volume 4 LIBI-MARY

Subjects

1. Lilye, William
2. Keyserling, Hermann
3. Infant Incubators
4. Harvesting Machinery
5. Karateghin

6. Ignatius
7. Liver and Gall Bladder Diseases
8. Indians of North America
9. Jewelry
10. Lowell, Institute

Answer Key: Exercise 1
1. X
2.
3. X
4.
5.
6. X
7. X
8. X

Exercise 2
1. 4
2. 3
3. 2
4. 1
5. 3
6. 2
7. 4
8. 2
9. 3
10. 4

233: The *Readers' Guide to Periodical Literature*

Purpose: To provide practice in interpreting information found in the *Readers' Guide to Periodical Literature*.

Introduction: If you were doing a report on a current subject, you would probably need to look up magazine articles that were written recently. An index that can help you to locate magazine articles is the *Readers' Guide to Periodical Literature*. The *Readers' Guide* lists the articles in alphabetical order by subject and gives you all the information you will need to look up the article (title of the article, name of the magazine, volume and page numbers, date of the magazine, etc.). However, since the names of the magazines and other information is given in an abbreviated form, you will need to refer to the list of abbreviations that is printed in the front of the *Readers' Guide*. By checking the abbreviation key, you will be sure that you are correctly identifying the periodical cited.

To find the subject you are researching in the *Readers' Guide*, you may have to check under several listings. For example, if you wanted to know about dune buggy races, you should check that subject heading first. If nothing is listed under that topic, you might try "races," "sports-racing," "racing," etc. You might find it listed under one of these related topics.

When searching for your subject, you will first want to use the unbound paperback issues of the *Readers' Guide* because they are the most current indexes. If you cannot find your information in these copies, then you will refer to the older, bound volumes.

Study the following sample entries from the *Readers' Guide*. Read the questions that follow and answer them on a separate sheet of paper.

Reference Material: Sample entries from the *Readers' Guide to Periodical Literature*

FIREFLIES

    Catching fireflies for profit. il Nat Geog World 38:20-1 Ag '78

    Facts about fireflies. il Natl Sci Digest 22:59-60 Jl '78

FIREWORKS

    Big blast. N Caplain. il Parents Mag 53: 64-67 My 15, '78

FIRST GRADE   See Education, Elementary.

Questions:

1. Under what subject heading would you find information concerning making money on fireflies?

2. What magazine contains an article entitled "Facts About Fireflies"?

3. What volume of *Parents Magazine* contains information on fireworks?

4. Where would you have to look to find information on the first grade in elementary school?

5. Which articles listed above are illustrated?

6. Which months are abbreviated in the articles listed above?

7. On what pages in *Parents Magazine* would you find information about fireworks?

Answer Key:

1. FIREFLIES

2. National Science Digest

3. Volume 53

4. Under the subject heading "Education, Elementary"

5. "Catching Fireflies for Profit," "Facts about Fireflies," and "Big Blast"

6. August, July, and May

7. Pages 64 to 67 of the May 15, 1978 issue

234: Maps

Purpose: To provide practice in interpreting information found on maps.

Introduction: When you travel in an unfamiliar part of the country, you will have to read a map to locate the correct route to your destination. Study the map below and on a separate sheet of paper answer the questions that follow.

Reference Material:

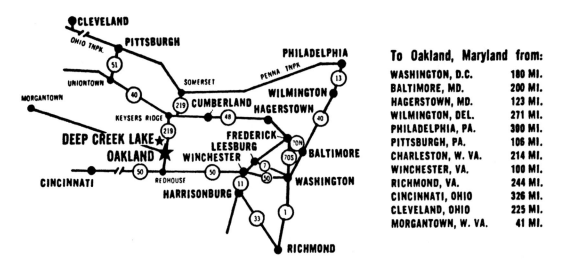

To Oakland, Maryland from:

WASHINGTON, D.C.	180 MI.
BALTIMORE, MD.	200 MI.
HAGERSTOWN, MD.	123 MI.
WILMINGTON, DEL.	271 MI.
PHILADELPHIA, PA.	300 MI.
PITTSBURGH, PA.	106 MI.
CHARLESTON, W. VA.	214 MI.
WINCHESTER, VA.	100 MI.
RICHMOND, VA.	244 MI.
CINCINNATI, OHIO	326 MI.
CLEVELAND, OHIO	225 MI.
MORGANTOWN, W. VA.	41 MI.

Questions:

1. What places are marked with stars on this map? Why?
2. If you lived in Cleveland, Ohio, how many miles would you have to travel to get to Oakland, Maryland?
3. If you lived in Baltimore, Maryland, and followed Routes 40 and 13 to Philadelphia, Pennsylvania, what direction according to a compass would you be traveling?
4. What routes would you follow from Richmond, Virginia, to get to Oakland, Maryland, in the shortest amount of time?
5. How many miles from Pittsburgh, Pennsylvania, is Oakland, Maryland?
6. Would you travel east or west from Uniontown, Pennsylvania, to get to Somerset, Pennsylvania?
7. What is the city that is furthest north on this map?
8. On what road is Hagerstown, Maryland, located?
9. What city is furthest away from Oakland, Maryland?
10. By looking at the map, which of the following cities is closest to Deep Creek Lake: Morgantown, Wilmington, Somerset?

Answer Key:

1. Deep Creek Lake and Oakland; They are probably places of special interest.
2. 225 miles
3. North
4. 33N, 11N, 50W, 219N
5. 106 miles
6. East
7. Cleveland
8. Route 48
9. Cincinnati, Ohio
10. Somerset

Printed in the United States
40336LVS00006BA/106